D1511745

THOMAS STROBL & MARTIN ZELLER

Freeclimbing

A COMPLETE GUIDE TO ROCK CLIMBING

WARD LOCK

Contents

The Sport of Freeclimbing

Since the 1970s, free-climbing has experienced an enormous upsurge of interest and achievement, with the number of active climbers and the general popularity of the sport growing at a tremendous rate. At the 1992 Winter Olympics in Albertville, sport climbing was included as a demonstration event for the first time. This rapid progress was possible because the climbing movement freed itself from the romantic attitude to mountaineers, to an emphasis on attaining alpine summits and of climbing as an opportunity to enjoy the outdoors. Over time, precise analysis of the complicated sequences of movements and the development of targeted training programmes have enabled climbers to achieve previously undreamt of levels of performance. As a result of these changes, the values of many climbers have changed. Lengthy ascents in the Alps are no longer the sole pinnacle of achievement and difficult climbs in lower mountain ranges have also, at last, been acknowledged as worthwhile feats. Climbing has become an end in itself, and is no longer just the skill required to ascend an alpine peak.

However, the reduction of mountain climbing to sheer "gymnastics on rock" certainly does not mean that freeclimbing is wholly devoid of flair. Quite the reverse: freeclimbing offers more scope than virtually any other sport for individual climbers to adapt it to their own requirements. Whether they choose to pit themselves against others in international competition in front of a large audience, to conquer a boulder-strewn cliff on a lonely beach in Corsica, to delight in the interaction of their own muscles on the artificial climbing wall in the local gym or to defy thin mountain air, extreme cold and enormous dangers in order to master routes of the utmost difficulty at heights of 6,000 metres in the Karakorum Mountains of Central Asia, all climbers need a foundation of knowledge, skill and technique from which to build and on which to practise.

On the cliffs of Sardinia

and the equipment needed. This will allow you to learn quickly, and thoroughly; then, as you gain more experience, you will be able to progress from climbing in low hills, to routes in more mountainous regions.

Finally, a few words on the term "freeclimbing". This term is often confused with "free solo" or "soloing", but freeclimbing, in fact, means rock climbing using ropes, nuts, bolts, pitons, etc. at one's discretion and for safety reasons. However, this equipment is not used as a direct aid to ascent.

Free solo or soloing, on the other hand, refers to rock climbing without any aids to safety at all so that the risk of a fall is enormous.

Freeclimbing is a dangerous sport. It must be emphasized that, at any level of activity, there is always a risk of severe injury or even death. Anyone wishing to participate in the sport is therefore urged in the strongest possible terms to undertake full professional tuition. In the course of such tuition, all risks and danger areas will be illustrated and the correct safety procedures learnt. The use of safety equipment is essential, because without the correct training you will be a danger not only to yourself but to others as well.

This book offers you a good introduction to the sport, to give you some idea of what it entails before you begin and to act as a reference as you learn and want to improve your knowledge and expertise. All aspects of freeclimbing are included in this book so that you can familiarize yourself with technical terms

History and Ethics

Climbing is a basic instinct for humans, whether it be to hunt for prey or to flee predators. Men and women, for the most part, no longer need to climb for either of these reasons. But the drive for supremacy over nature has been both man's triumph and his folly through the centuries, and the history of the world charts his predatory conquests and submissions.

Similarly, the history of climbing has been largely one of conquest of high mountain peaks and, as with territorial conquests or political subjection the only rules are those made by the conquerors themselves. Mountaineers adhere to their own particular code of ethics and this explains why the codes governing climbing styles have varied immensely from one generation to another, and even more from one country to another. But despite this, today, there are still no rules or criteria laid down by official bodies, just codes of ethics supported by climbers themselves and developed over the long history of the sport. The history of climbing begins around the middle of the sixteenth century when the conquest of the Alps was well in hand. At this time, Dr Paccard and Jacques Balmat succeeded in climbing the highest mountain in the Alps, Mont Blanc although it was the development of an interest in science and geology that provided the initial impetus for these conquests. But, by the middle of the nineteenth century, the Alps had become a playground for the upper classes. Among their number was a band of committed climbers with sufficient means to finance their "peak bagging" expeditions. The difficulties they encountered were great, particularly considering their equipment, clothing and general

West wall of Bloßstock VII b (UIAA VI)
Rudolf Klemm and companions 19. 3. 1916

knowledge of mountains. The style of these ascents is fairly well documented, although in many cases the exact truth remains hidden. For most, the tactics were open and ruthless, and a summit would be gained by any possible means. The climbers would set off across the glaciers, led by local professional guides who carried most of the loads. If these climbers had had the benefit of the lightweight materials used today, they would have been used high on the mountain, like the ladders employed for negotiating crevasses. As it was, anything went: metal pegs, wooden wedges and ice axes were all employed, although the primitive nature of the equipment available meant that even these aids did little to reduce the enormous challenge of climbing a peak 4500 m high. The only ethic adhered to in those days was to be absolutely honest in your claim that you had reached the summit, and to pay the guides their wages, with a bonus for a successful conquest.

In essence, the development of freeclimbing was not a major innovation. If there were

plenty of holds, these pioneering mountaineers used them; if not, they simply aided their way up. What made a huge difference was that climbers started looking for new conquests. They found the new challenges they were seeking on large faces of steep rock, where they could test and extend their skills in a way that removed the need to complete the rest of the route to the summit. The recorded history of rock climbing dates from the late nineteenth century, and is well documented in many European countries. In a sense, it was a cheaper alternative to mountaineering. Most of the early climbing was entirely free of climbing aids, simply because climbers soloed, and the routes never presented any real difficulty. This was perhaps just as well, since protection equipment was virtually non-existent: there were no strong anchors and the hemp ropes then in use provided moral support but little else, since the impact force exerted during a long fall would have broken the rope.

In the United Kingdom, freeclimbing became an extension of soloing, but with a group of two or more the range of possibilities was extended. The concept of not damaging the rock was paramount, and the notion of progressing upwards without aids was fundamental. However, there were two exceptions. Firstly, it was quite permissible to stand on a partner's shoulders, and even greater advantage could be gained from bringing a third person in on the act: a party of three could get some 5 m up a blank wall. Secondly, the rope could be used as a tool; the technique of lassoing a high spike of rock became an essential art when faced with a holdless wall, and pulling up on a threaded pebble placed in a crack was considered inge-

nious. However, the placing of any metal spikes in the rock was absolutely forbidden: engineering on the crag was not allowed.

Freeclimbing also started to develop in certain parts of Germany. In 1908 Rudolf Ehrmann wrote a guide to the sandstone outcrops of the Elbe Valley near Dresden in Saxony. He laid down rules for the ascent of rock faces without the use of fixed aids, which still constitute the accepted code of ethics today. The two basic rules were that no aids to ascent could be used at all and that any protection used had to be placed on ascent only. Since the soft sandstone offered few natural spikes, it was drilled to accept metal pitons.

In Germany, therefore, rock climbing was free and totally safe, while in Britain it was almost free and quite dangerous. In 1936 the two cultures clashed angrily in North Wales. The banging of metal against metal was heard on Tryfan, a Welsh mountain. Later on, Herr Teufel and Herr Sedymayr announced the new Munich Climb, with two points of aid. The route was promptly climbed free without

the pitons, which were removed and no doubt posted back to Germany. Such events, involving the best climbers of the day, shaped the ethics of the time.

After the Second World War, ironmongery such as pitons, karabiners and bolts of all descriptions came into widespread use as climbing standards rose around the world. The ethical code based on the use of natural protection faded into the background, and the metal piton became the standard form of protection at the crux points on hard climbs: nothing was to get in the way of climbing development. However, things started to come full circle with the use of lightweight aluminium to produce some ingenious protection devices. The invention that changed the face of freeclimbing in the 1970s was the "Friend", the brainchild of an American climber called Ray Jardine and had the added

Above: Climbing with artificial aids
Left: Stefan Glowacz in Desert Gold, Red Rocks, USA. First ascent, 5.13a, in the clean climbing style

Equipping a sport climbing route in the Frankenjura, Bavaria

bonus of being light enough to carry on the route; it had four cams which expanded at a logarithmic rate, so they would grip in a parallel crack. Previously, only a piton could do this. The Friend captured the imagination of all other leading climbers and allowed freeclimbing to become a relatively safe sport. Climbers now faced the challenge of ridding all climbs of permanent protection. In America, the hairline cracks produced by the placement of pitons had opened up to such an extent that they were wide enough to be used as finger holds. This resulted in the creation of some of the longest freeclimbing routes in the world and the 900m aid climbs of the 1960s have now been climbed entirely free. In the Yosemite valley of California, however, aid climbing is still thriving and is just as dangerous as ever. It should still be given due respect, but its merits and techniques lie outside the scope of this book.

Freeclimbing was introduced into France in the mid-1970s, principally by the British climber Pete Livesey. However, the French limestone cliffs offer little natural protection and have no cracks in which Friends can be placed. Consequently, the French adopted the resin bolt as a means of protection. The discipline that emerged became known as sport climbing, and it is French climbers who set world sport climbing standards.

One rock type, sandstone, deserves a mention in any history of freeclimbing as it is too brittle to offer much natural protection but is covered in an abundance of finger-sized holds and its faces are often low enough for a rope to be dropped from the top of a route. For these reasons, sandstone has always attracted freeclimbers and, today, just outside Paris, in the Forest of Fontainebleau, there are thousands of sandstone boulders, and the exploits of accomplished "boulderers" in this Parisian playground have always set the standards for freeclimbers throughout the world.

Manfred Eichhorn on the "Desaster" route (X) on the Bärenschluchtwände

Ever since climbing developed as a sport, climbers have compared climbs for difficulty and seriousness. Eventually, such attempts at comparison gave rise to grading systems, with routes being allocated grades on a scale of seriousness. Initially, the scale was quite a simple one, ranging from Easy through Moderate and Hard to Difficult. By the turn of the century, however, standards had risen so dramatically that the term "Severe" was added to describe a climb more challenging than "Difficult", and possibly even dangerous. By the 1990s there were nine grades within the Extremely Severe category. On small outcrops of rock, where a rope could be used to protect climbers from above, a numbering system was used to grade the technical diffi-

UIAA scale	France	USA	England		Australia	Former GDR
VI +	6 a	5.10 a	5 b	E 2	19	VII c
VII −	6 b	5.10 b			20	VIII a
VII		5.10 c	5 c		21	VIII b
VII +	6 c	5.10 d		E 3	21	
		5.11 a			22	VIII c
VIII −	7 a	5.11 b	6 a		23	IX a
VIII		5.11 c		E 4	24	IX b
		5.11 d			25	IX c
VIII +	7 b	5.12 a	6 b		26	X a
IX −		5.12 b		E 5		
	7 c	5.12 c			27	
IX		5.12 d	6 c		28	
		5.13 a		E 6	29	X b
IX +	8 a	5.13 b				
X −		5.13 c			30	
		5.13 d	7 a		31	
X	8 b	5.14 a		E 7	32	
X +		5.14 b	7 b			X c
XI −	8 c	5.14 c			33	

culty of a route, bearing in mind the size of holds, steepness and the general skills needed to climb it. This system used the numbers 1–5, and often a letter as well (a, b or c) to denote its level more precisely.

All across Europe, numbering systems developed quite separately from each other. The system that emerged in Britain factored an assessment of seriousness into the rating, which now precedes the standard technical rating. Thus a VS 5a rating would indicate a seriousness rating of Very Severe and a technical difficulty of 5a. The two ratings have worked well in tandem. In the USA, numbers are also used, but decimal points are preferred to letters. Strangely, no one has been able to accept that a climb can be grade 6, so 5.10, 5.11, etc. are used instead. In France, the safety aspect led to an explosion of standards which has now reached grade 9. With each country having its own climbing ethics and styles, it has been impossible to arrive at a uniform standard. However, most countries now give a French grade in order to aid comparisons.

Despite these rules and performance-oriented assessment systems, some of which sound really dogmatic, each individual climber can choose either to follow the rules as laid down or to practise the sport as he or she sees fit. Nobody is in a position to enforce any particular set of regulations. However, any attempt to compare achievements must be based on honesty. Even though it is virtually impossible to monitor an ascent made without artificial aids in a remote alpine region, black sheep in the climbing community are always unmasked sooner or later. So have the courage of your convictions.

Sport climbing: styles of ascent

On sight: *To lead a climb with no falls without ever having seen the route before. It is permissible to consider the route from below but not to watch another climber ascending it.*

Flash: *To lead a climb with no falls on a previously unattempted route. In this case, the climber may abseil down the face in order to inspect it before the ascent, or she may watch someone else climbing it.*

Redpoint: *To lead a climb in one go without falling. All protection must be placed from the climbing position. In this case, it does not matter how often the route has been attempted in the past.*

Pinkpoint (en libre): *To lead a climb in one go without falls, with protection put in place beforehand.*

Red circle: *After a fall from the leading position, the climber does not abseil down and start all over again from the bottom, but rather returns to the last "no hand rest" (a place where it is possible to stand up without holding on) and starts to climb again. She is then protected from the top until she reaches the topmost anchor.*

Top rope: *To ascend a route with rope protection from the top.*

Free solo: *To climb a route without any rope protection. Freeclimbing is often confused, wrongly, with free solo.*

All free: *The anchors on a route are used not as a means of progression but just for resting.*

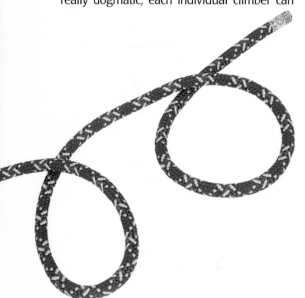

Protecting the Environment

Despite the huge increase in recent years in the use of artificial climbing walls, climbing is still, for most people, an outdoor sport. Intensive encounters with nature are important for an understanding of the natural world and foster the development of one's personality. However, the rock face that, for climbers, is an item of sports equipment, is also a very sensitive ecosystem, so conflict between users of nature and protectors of nature is unavoidable.

Apart from the Alps, the areas most affected by human intrusion are lower mountain ranges up to about 2000 metres in height. Until now, nobody was interested in these areas, since no economic use had been found for them. As a result, these unspoilt yet neglected landscapes became the last retreat for many plant and animal species. Moreover, their extreme locations offer extraordinary conditions for specialized plant species that have been confined to such locations since the last ice age.

Although people have been climbing in these areas for more than a hundred years, significant environmental problems have emerged only in the last few decades. As a result of widespread environmental pollution, caused particularly by pesticides and other toxic substances, some species of birds of prey were already threatened with extinction as early as 1950, before climbers had had any significant effect on the environment. The toxic substances accumulated in such large quantities in the bodies of the birds (which stood at the end of a lengthy food chain) that they could no longer reproduce and thus were no longer able to survive as a species.

The freeclimbing boom of the last decade has led to a drastic increase in the number of climbers and the opening up of freeclimbing routes on virtually every available rock face. Even in the remotest areas, countless enthusiasts are now to be found every few metres inching their way up a crag. Unless climbers behave responsibly, such an onslaught can easily give rise to irreparable environmental damage and unnecessary conflict with other interest groups and residents. The most serious negative effects of climbing on the environment can be divided into five categories:

1. The tramping of feet on approaches and descent routes, on ledges or in cracks and fissures displaces delicate plants and eventually gives rise to erosion. This also removes the vegetation on which some species feed, particularly insects. The pruning and clearing of routes, during which all vegetation and soil is removed from crags in order to facilitate climbing quickly leads to the total destruction of the flora of steep rock faces.
2. The disturbance and displacement of animal species that depend on steep crags for survival. Birds of prey, such as the peregrine falcon and the eagle owl, already threatened with extinction, are particularly badly affected, especially when they are looking for a breeding place and when the young are being hatched and reared.
3. Rubbish and excrement upsets the ecological balance of remote areas.
4. Noise nuisance, inconsiderate parking, rough camping and many other bad habits give rise to social conflict.
5. Daubing crags with route names and chalk, and leaving pegs hammered into the rock, are sometimes – quite rightly – regarded as disfigurement of the landscape.

Inadequate information and lack of understanding of environmental issues often lead to inappropriate behaviour on the part of climbers, the consequences of which can sometimes be extreme. In many places in the lower mountain ranges of Germany, environmental damage has led to extensive bans on climbing. And in other areas, such as the

Practice crags are often the last retreats for rare

A total ban on climbing is the last resort

...imal and plant species

South of France, intolerable conditions for residents have meant that whole areas have been closed to climbers. On the other hand, one sometimes gets the impression that this situation is sometimes exploited by interested parties. So while entire river landscapes not far from climbing areas have been destroyed by the construction of canals and other environmental abominations committed for economic reasons are tolerated or even encouraged, the authorities have tended on occasions to impose unnecessarily draconian climbing bans in order to demonstrate their environmental credentials.

For these reasons, national associations such as the British Mountaineering Council in the UK and the Access Fund in the USA are working to resolve such conflicts and to protect the

Lack of regard for the environment

are being affixed at the end of routes. After completing their ascent, climbers can use these lower-off points to abseil/rappel back down the route they have just climbed. In this way, they can avoid trampling the sensitive flora on the tops of cliffs.

All national climbing organizations and associations are well aware of the impact of climbers to the environment and have issued lists of sensible guidelines. These vary from country to country and cover a multitude of topics. They should serve to increase awareness of environmental issues among climbers and to remind them that they are not the only ones who wish to enjoy the countryside.

natural environment. They are seeking to enter into dialogue with official bodies and nature conservation groups in order to ease tensions and to represent the interests of climbers. On the one hand, nature conservancy measures are being developed and implemented, while on the other, education and information programmes are being put in place in order to encourage climbers to behave in an environmentally sensitive way. In areas at great risk from environmental damage, protected areas are being established. These may be individual sections of rock faces, individual crags or even entire rock massifs. Apart from a few total, all-year-round climbing bans, these protected areas are usually closed to climbers from 1 February to 30 June, the period when the birds that breed on the crags are looking for nesting places and are hatching and rearing their young. The closure of such areas is drawn to climbers' attention in specialist magazines, in leaflets and on information boards at the sites in question. In order to avoid further closures and restrictions, these bans should be respected wherever they are introduced. Environmentally conscious climbers are also trying to prevent erosion by repairing and relaying footpaths. So-called "lower offs"

Considerate climbing

1. Try to share transport to and from climbing areas in order to reduce the volume of traffic

2. Park with respect and consideration for residents and other users

3. Use approved footpaths only, even if you have to walk further as a result

4. Keep your belongings near you at all times

5. Use lower-off points at all times

6. Treat the cliff surroundings with care and take litter away with you

7. Enquire about any temporary climbing bans

8. Observe all local restrictions

9. In order to avoid damage to the environment, do not lower off on soft rock

10. Use soft footwear on sandstone

11. Only abseil in designated areas

Equipment

Equipment plays an important role in all aspects of freeclimbing, except the free solo style when protection is eschewed altogether, because freeclimbers entrust their lives to ropes, karabiners, harnesses (items of equipment used to support the climber in the event of a fall) and all the other elements in the safety chain. It is important, therefore, to acquire a high level of specialist knowledge of equipment in order to ensure your own and others' safety.

The UIAA (Union Internationale des Associations d'Alpinisme), in collaboration with many other national standards committees, has developed standards that lay down minimum requirements for the suitability and safety of a piece of equipment. The UIAA or DIN (German standards) label is proof that a particular item of equipment meets the minimum safety requirements, but certainly cannot be taken as proof that the item is also suitable for freeclimbing. The standards themselves do not necessarily take account of the differing requirements of the various kinds of mountain sports, which range from glacier hiking to competition climbing. Consequently it is often not so easy to put together a suitable rack, both because of the enormous range of goods on offer, usually promoted by glossy advertising making extravagant promises, and because of the somewhat confusing maze of standards that apply to climbing equipment. The next few pages contain essential information and tips that will guide you in the purchase of individual items, but always seek expert advice when you are unsure.

Footwear

Function:
▶ to establish optimal contact between foot and rock;
▶ to prevent slipping or sliding on even the smallest uneven patches through high friction;
▶ to protect the foot from injury.

The most important item of equipment for a free climber is the shoe. Stiff mountain boots with hard, treaded soles have proved to be utterly unsuitable for use as climbing shoes, so anyone wishing just to dabble a little in the sport would be well advised to use tightly fitting plimsolls with smooth soles. Nowadays light, relatively soft shoes with smooth soles made of a special rubber are considered ideal, and a wide range of such shoes is now available.

Three factors determine the qualities of a climbing shoe:

1. The lateral and longitudinal stiffness of the sole.

▶ Soft soles: good frictional qualities that allow maximum contact between shoe and rock; however, edge stability is generally lower and they tend to wear out fairly quickly.

▶ Hard soles: energy-saving when standing on small footholds; edge stability is high and they tend to last longer.

2. Shape of the upper.

▶ Ankle-high shoe: good protection for the foot with greater support for the ankle (energy-saving).

▶ Low shoe: good freedom of movement around the ankle with adequate support for the foot.

▶ Slipper (extremely light and soft, usually a slip-on design): allows excellent conformation of the entire foot to even the slightest uneven patches on the rock, but very energy-sapping as a result.

3. Fit.

The shoe or boot must fit very precisely if it is to transfer energy from the foot to the rock as efficiently as possible. There should not be even a millimetre of free space in the shoe, and even after long periods of standing on the balls of the feet, the shoe should not twist at all. As a result, most freeclimbers quickly become real masochists and buy their climbing footwear several sizes too small. This has the effect of pushing the toes upwards, thus allowing energy to be transferred more efficiently to the tip of the shoe.

In order to concentrate the power to be transferred on the tip of the big toe, which is obviously the strongest of the five, a shoe with an asymmetrical section has been developed. In such a shoe, the tip of the big toe fits snugly into the tip of the shoe. In a shoe with a symmetrical section, the tip of the shoe is in line with the central axis of the shoe.

Climbing with symmetrical shoes is somewhat less energy-sapping than with asymmetrical shoes, since the load is distrib-

Example of a slipper, low shoe and high shoe

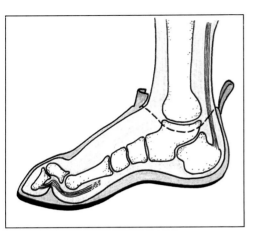

Toes curled up in climbing shoe

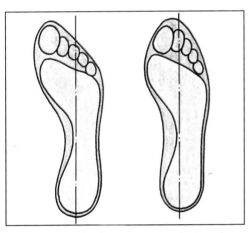

Asymmetrical (left), and symmetrical section

uted more evenly between all the toes. On the very smallest footholds, however, the asymmetrical shape, with its added grip, comes into its own. You should always make sure that the tip of the shoe is as flat as possible, so that advantage can be taken of even the smallest holes and the narrowest of cracks in the rock.

Applications

Walking boots with hard soles and big deep treads do not offer any support to the foot and are considered unsuitable for freeclimbing.
Ankle high and low shoe with medium-soft soles have proved to be the styles with the widest sphere of application. Although for those who are new to the sport of freeclimbing, the more comfortable symmetrical shape will be adequate. As your performance level increases, you will probably choose to wear asymmetric shoes with a considerably tighter fit. They are ideal for most freeclimbing routes on practice crags, in alpine regions and on artificial climbing walls.

Extremely soft slippers are well suited to shorter routes or bouldering; however, they should only be used by climbers who have already developed a good technique.

Hints on buying
When buying climbing shoes, remember that the uppers, which are usually of suede, will stretch a little in use, so choose a slightly smaller size than you would normally buy. There are often considerable differences between the sizes used by the various manufacturers, so it is a good idea to try a range of different brands in order to find the one that fits best. Before the shoes are used for climbing, you should allow them to mould to the shape of your foot by walking and climbing in them on easy terrain. This process can be aided by wetting the shoes slightly so that they dry to the shape of your foot.

Despite the fact that this section has emphasized the need for the closest fit possible, it should be remembered that permanent damage can be caused to the foot by wearing shoes that are extremely small.

Harnesses

Function:
▶ to transfer the loads generated in a fall as comfortably as possible to the body;
▶ to make dangling on the rope a relatively comfortable procedure;
▶ to make handy attachment points for climbing gear such as karabiners, slings, etc.

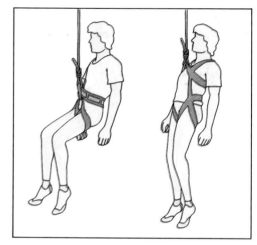

Sit harness (left) and full-body harness

There are standards for harnesses (DIN 7947, UIAA), but the fact that a particular piece of equipment conforms to one of them says nothing at all about its suitability for free-climbing.

There are five different types of harness on the market:
▶ sit harness (sport climbing harness): well suited;
▶ light chest harness: well suited;
▶ conventional sit harness: not well suited;
▶ conventional chest harness: less well suited;
▶ full-body harness: not well suited.

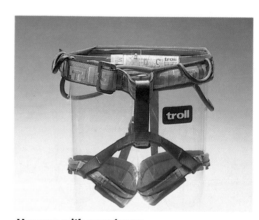

Harness with gear loops

The harness best suited to freeclimbing is a combined sit and light chest harness. Conventional sit harnesses and full-body harnesses are less comfortable when dangling on the end of a rope and are more suited for use on glacier routes, mountain climbs or very easy rock climbing routes. There is nothing wrong with conventional chest harnesses, but they are heavier and more expensive.

Full-body harnesses and sit harnesses must basically be used on their own while chest harnesses and conventional sit harnesses should always be used in combination.

Lightweight competition harness

Sit harness (sport climbing harness)

The principle on which sit harnesses are constructed means that the loads generated by a fall are transmitted in the first instance to the thighs, where they are partially absorbed by the process of drawing the knees up to the body and then transferred to the rest of the body. With conventional climbing harnesses, on the other hand, such loads are transmitted directly to the spinal column. With sit harnesses, the climber can dangle from the end of a rope in a comfortable sitting position, while with conventional harnesses the dangling position is an upright one, in which the leg loops and chest harness can cut painfully into the climber's body (see diagram p. 22). A sit harness consists of two parts, the waist belt and the leg loops. The waist belt and leg loops can be joined at the front with a central "tie-in" loop and buckle, or they may be left separate. In the first case, the harness is self-supporting, i.e. it sits tightly against the body even when the rope is not threaded. In the second case, the waist belt and leg loops must be joined by a rope or a separate "tie-in" loop, so that the harness does not slide off. While these harnesses are somewhat lighter and cheaper, they are neither as comfortable nor as durable.

Hints on buying

Choose a waist belt on which the padding material is spaced at intervals of between 5 and 20 cm. There are two different shapes of leg loop, O-loops and V-loops. O-loops are more comfortable, provided that they are an exact fit. To check, stand up and flex your thigh muscles: if there is just enough room to get your hand through the loop, then the fit is perfect. You need have no qualms about buying V-loops in a slightly larger size. Their sizing is less specific (for thick or thin clothing), but they are not quite so comfortable.

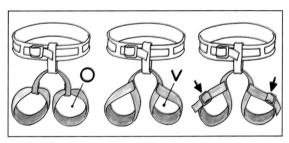

Examples of leg loops. From the left: O-shaped, V-shaped and adjustable leg loops

There are also adjustable leg loops, which are particularly useful on alpine routes, where the clothing you need to wear varies considerably with the weather. Some manufacturers sell separate waist belts and leg loops so that a climber can easily select exactly the right fit for both parts of the body, particularly if he or she is not exactly a standard size. This is especially important for women, particularly for the fitting of the belt around their hips, as manufacturers generally size their equipment for men.

The comfort of a harness in the dangling position can only be judged by dangling in it for at least ten minutes. Neither the existence of padding nor its thickness is necessarily any guarantee of a comfortable harness where the straps do not cut into the skin. Such tests have often revealed tightly pressing metal buckles as the cause of much pain and discomfort.

Finally, note carefully the placement and design of the gear loops as their position and material are both important. Make sure they provide sufficient room for arranging protection equipment so that it is clearly visible and is easily to hand. The material used to make the loops should also be of sufficient thickness to prevent the ends of the gates on karabiners from snagging on them.

Light chest harness

A light chest harness is an unpadded harness in a figure-of-eight shape. It is available in fixed-size or adjustable models.

Hints on buying

The two front loops should just touch when in position on your chest. Here again, it is important to test the harness (for straps that pinch and buckles that cut the flesh) by hanging from each harness in turn.

Chest harnesses are very controversial items. On the one hand, the DIN and UIAA standards stipulate the wearing of a chest harness, while on the other, the climbing fraternity, to say nothing of virtually all freeclimbers, wear a sit harness for protection, dispensing altogether with the chest harness.

Sit harnesses take up the entire force generated by a fall. A chest harness, however, merely maintains the climber in an upright position during a fall and while he or she is dangling. For this reason, only a light, figure-of-eight chest harness is necessary.

However, before choosing a harness, remember that it has been established that the risk of serious injury to the spinal column during a fall is very high if a climber tilts backwards which is only possible in a seat harness. The risk is all the greater the longer the fall, the less controlled it is and the less accomplished the climber's falling technique. If the climber is wearing a heavy rucksack the risk becomes even greater and then a chest harness becomes essential, even for professionals. A chest harness can be dispensed with only if falls are likely to be short and controllable, if the climber is not carrying a rucksack and if he or she has learnt how to fall properly.

Harness life and care

A harness can normally be expected to last for about five years. Simpler harnesses made of less expensive materials or those in frequent

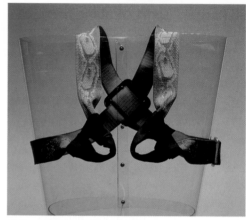

Adjustable light chest harness

use may last one or two years less. The harness should be carefully inspected at regular intervals, and after serious falls, for damage and wear at the seams and on the fabric. It should be replaced if necessary. To maintain the quality of the harness, keep it away from any strong chemicals and clean in a weak, lukewarm soap solution. As with all nylon products, it should be stored in a dark, dry, well-ventilated place.

Helmets

Function:
- ▶ to protect the head from falling rocks;
- ▶ to protect the head during falls.

There is a DIN and UIAA standard for helmets as well. It stipulates that the energy of a falling stone should be absorbed elastically by the helmet. For this reason, the helmet does not sit directly on top of the head but is kept at a distance of 2 to 4 cm from the skull by webbing straps. In the event of an impact, the dome of the helmet deforms and the webbing straps stretch as they absorb the kinetic energy of the falling rock.

Hints on buying
Apart from making sure the helmet carries a

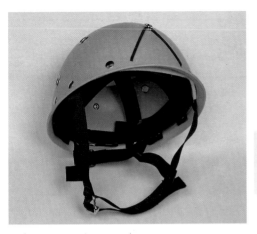

Lightweight helmet with webbing straps

DIN or UIAA label, the most important thing is to be certain that it is a good fit. You must be able to adjust the inner and chin straps on the helmet so that under no circumstances (e.g. while scraping along a rock face) can the dome be pushed backwards to expose the vulnerable upper forehead.

The following factors are important for comfort and safety:

- an unrestricted field of vision;
- bright colours and adequate ventilation (adequate distance between the head and the ventilation holes) in order to prevent a build-up of heat;
- low weight (lightweight helmets weigh between 400 and 500 g).

Like light chest harnesses, helmets are controversial. In virtually all photographs of freeclimbers, the only headgear sported by the open-air acrobats is a casual headband. And yet helmets can save lives. They can be dispensed with only if rock falls can be completely ruled out and only short, controlled falls are likely. On alpine routes and routes that end on a terrace of scree material or skirt areas of crumbling rock, a helmet is absolutely essential; and if you have not yet fully mastered the technique of falling, then you should most certainly wear a helmet, since it significantly reduces the risk of serious head injuries.

Ropes

Function:
- to hold a climber in the event of the worst possible fall.

The ropes in common use today, which are also subject to a DIN/UIAA standard, are of Kernmantel construction. The load-bearing core is surrounded by a protective sheath that absorbs only a small part of the energy when the rope comes under strain. The force exerted by a falling climber may not exceed a certain maximum value in order to avoid injury. For this reason, the maximum force that is allowed to be tolerated by the body has been set at 12 kN. In order that this maximum value cannot be exceeded, the climbing ropes stretch in order to absorb part of the fall energy. However, they should not stretch too far, otherwise the fall distance would be extended unnecessarily.

The most important technical measurements for a rope are diameter, weight and the number of UIAA standard falls it can sustain. A standard fall is a precisely defined, carefully standardized simulation of a severe fall during which an object weighing 80 or 50 kg is attached to the rope and dropped from a specified height. Depending on the type of rope, the standard stipulates that a rope should survive a

1. Single rope: *These are mainly used on sport climbing routes, and are between 10 and 11mm in diameter. A lot of the top sports climbers are incredibly light, so will be safe on a 10 mm rope; for heavier climbers a thicker rope is a very wise precaution. Most sport climbs have a belay at 30 m, so a 60 m length is essential.*

2. Double rope: *Here, two 8.8mm or 9mm diameter ropes are popular, again for lightweight and heavier climbers. They are not as strong as a single rope, and are intended to work together. Even so, one is nearly always strong enough on its own, though particular caution should be taken where a long dynamic fall has occurred. A 50–55 m length is normal for double ropes, as two 60 m lengths would weigh too much at the end of the climb.*

3. Static rope: *This is often known as caving rope. It is 10 mm in diameter and does not stretch. It must not be used for dynamic lead climbing, but is very useful on crags for top-roping, indoor top-roping and supporting beginners from rope stretch.*

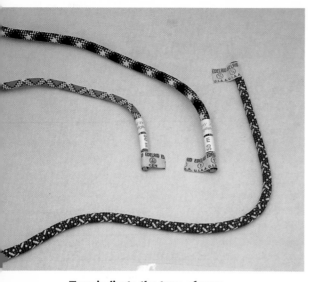

Tags indicate the type of rope

minimum of five or twelve such falls without breaking, although many ropes perform considerably better than the minimum. The number of standard falls a rope survives can be used to derive its capacity to absorb energy and, indirectly, its expected life. The impact force often quoted in descriptions of ropes is the force that would be exerted on a climber's body during a standard fall. As already mentioned, it may not exceed 12 kN. The lower the impact force, the more fall energy the rope absorbs, but the more a rope will stretch as it absorbs that energy.

Ropes are generally divided into three types:
1. single rope
2. double rope
3. static rope.

Each new climbing rope is easily identifiable by a tag attached to the end of the rope. There should also be a specification to support the tag, which will list all the technical requirements for holding dynamic falls. Sailing rope, which can look similar, is very strong but does not possess the greater dynamic properties of these three types of rope.

Both single and double ropes have advantages and disadvantages. On the whole double ropes are safer and should be used wherever possible. However, the techniques needed to use a double rope are complicated, and two different colours are essential to facilitate handling. They are also, of course, a more expensive option, since two ropes have to be purchased. In practice, however, most climbers buy just one and rely on their climbing partner to supply the second length. Single ropes, on the other hand, are lighter and easier to handle, and also less expensive. They have become very popular in sport climbing, where protection is guaranteed. Many climbers use an 11 mm rope for practising routes on which they are likely to fall frequently, subjecting the rope to a great deal of wear and tear. They may also have a new 10 mm rope for redpointing. Ropes generally do not break, as they have an immense capacity to withstand load, but they can be cut as they pass over sharp edges when under load.

Applications

As already noted, it is safer to use double ropes, both for ascending and descending. But when you lead a climb without artificial protection, you will almost certainly have to take a zigzag path up the rock face. Protection points are likely to be awkwardly arranged, and using only one rope will create a great deal of drag. With a double-rope system, the climber clips into alternate runners with each rope, thereby subjecting each one to fewer bends. The two ropes will then run more or less parallel up the cliff, considerably reducing the amount of drag. Even more importantly, a double-rope system provides additional protection in the event of a fall. Runners are designed to withstand a downward load; when the rope running through the top runner goes tight under load, the tensioned rope passing through the other runners will cause them to be pulled in a horizontal direction. This may pluck out a number of runners, and if the top one should then fail, the length of fall will be considerably increased. In this event, having two independent systems reduces the risk of serious injury. Both in the USA and UK, where protection placed and removed during the course of the climb is regarded as ethical on certain types of rock, it is advisable to use double ropes. Furthermore, you will have the use of two lengths of rope for the descent, which can often be very important where there are long distances between abseil points.

Ropes in use on a rockface

Rope lengths

Over the last 15 years, rope lengths have been subject to considerable inflationary pressures. From an average length of around 40 m, they have now settled down at around 50 to 60 m. Most freeclimbing routes are now being set up with these lengths in mind, and the number of routes that can be climbed with one 60 m top rope (p. 99) is increasing all the time.

Waterproofing

Many ropes are now given a water-resistant coating by the manufacturer, which is basically not necessary for freeclimbing routes on rock faces. Only when the ropes are to be used in ice or snow or on long alpine routes where there is a high risk or sudden rain or snowstorms is waterproofing useful. Some manufacturers claim that the coating they use reduces abrasion on the rock and thus protects the fibres of the outer sheath. On the other hand, some uncoated ropes handle better and have less of a tendency to kink.

Rope life and care

Rope life is a much debated topic. The most recent investigation by the DAV (German Alpine Club) safety committee has led to a change of opinion: nowadays ropes break only if they are lying across a sharp edge with a climber's weight on them. Since such situations do not occur on freeclimbing routes, which are usually vertical or overhanging, and since severe falls are a rare occurrence, ropes can be used safely until the outer sheath is visibly damaged. Tests have shown that the ropes that are not put under strain when lying across a sharp edge can survive considerably more than 200 typical freeclimbing falls. Even the ageing of the nylon, which used to be put forward as a reason why all ropes had to be changed every two to three years, even if not in use, has proved not to be a problem. However, if rock edges enter the equation, which is usu-

ally the case in alpine regions, then ageing has a considerable effect on the safety of a rope. Even with a rope straight from the factory, there can be no guarantee that it will hold every time it comes under strain while lying across a sharp edge. The safety qualities of a rope deteriorate as the total distance over which it has been used increases, and top-roping and abseiling put particularly heavy strains on a rope. Even the different kinds of rock, which range from smooth limestone to sharp-edged basic rock, such as basalt, have differing effects on the safety qualities of a rope. The safety committee of the German Alpine Club has depicted the performance of double ropes in the form of a curve representing the relationship between the total distance over which a rope has been used and safety performance when the rope is taut over a sharp edge of rock. With multi-fall and single ropes of smaller diameter, performance is reduced correspondingly. It can be seen from the curve that after a rope has been used over just 10,000 metres (equivalent to about 15 shorter alpine climbs with abseiling), its safety performance falls to 30 per cent of that of a new rope. This information does not in itself tell us when the time has come to change a rope, or to stop using it on climbs during which it might come under strain over a sharp edge. However, a rope should always be discarded if the outer sheath is visibly damaged, after it has been hit by falling rocks and after it has arrested a fall while lying over a sharp edge.

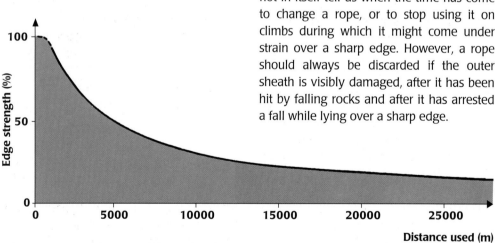

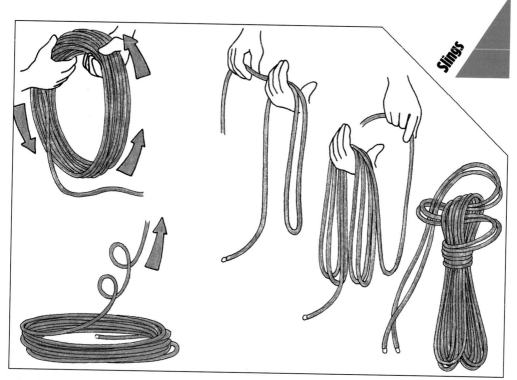

The right (top left) and wrong (below left) way to uncoil a rope, the mountaineer's coil (right)

The best place to store a rope is in a dry, dark, well-ventilated place, well away from any chemicals. Over time, dirt and grit will work their way into the outer sheath and weaken it. It is a good idea, therefore, to wash the rope occasionally in lukewarm water. Leave it to dry afterwards in a shady place, not in the sun, in a tumble dryer or over a radiator. A rope's tendency to kink depends mainly on the way it is handled. A rope kinks when it is bent back on itself. A rope with a lot of kinks in it is barely useable, and the climber's safety is often severely compromised as a result. Even a brand-new rope must be run out properly. If it is uncoiled layer by layer, each layer will have a twist in it. It follows from this that a rope must also be coiled without twists in it. One way of doing this is the mountaineer's coil method. To uncoil the rope again, untie it and lay it on the ground.

Slings

Function:
- ▶ when using karabiners, they act as a flexible link between the anchor on the rock and the rope;
- ▶ they ensure the rope runs straight, thereby minimizing rope drag;
- ▶ make it possible to use natural features (spikes of rock, threads, trees, etc.) as anchors;
- ▶ often used as belay anchors;
- ▶ used as attachment loops for various purposes (chest harness, sit harness, etc.).

There is also a standard for sewn slings, which must have a breaking strain of at least 22 kN. They are usually constructed of nylon, although slings made with "Dyneema" and "Spectra" have been available for some time. These slings have a considerably higher breaking strain than nylon versions, but they are more expensive, and since nylon slings fulfil their function extremely well, they will continue to dominate the market.

Types of tape

The tape used to make slings can either be of flat or tubular construction. As the name suggests, flat slings are usually somewhat inflexible, flat tape loops. The alternative and more popular tubular loops, on the other hand, look like ironed or flattened tubes and are very soft and flexible.

Tape that conforms to the standard must have stripes running lengthways woven into the reverse side so that its strength can be assessed, each stripe indicates a breaking strain of 5 kN.

Sling shapes

Slings also come in two shapes: circular slings and "quickdraws", which are straight in the middle with a loop at either end. You can make slings yourself from the tape available by the metre in specialist shops by tying them together with the special sling knots shown on p. 69. At least 10 cm of tape must be left free at either end and secured with adhesive tape. With quick-draws, the two end loops are formed by securing the larger loop with adhesive tape at both ends.

However, because of their greater strength (one knot reduces the breaking strain by 10 to 30 per cent), ready-sewn slings are highly recommended. The absence of a knot makes it less bulky as well as more secure since the knot and the string cannot work loose. When buying a ready-made sling, make sure that the seams have been sewn with a thread that differs in colour from the tape, so that slight wear can be detected easily.

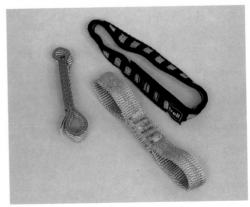

Quickdraws made of Dyneema (l.) and nylon (m.), circular slings made of nylon (r.)

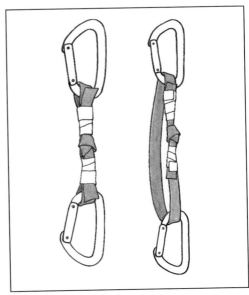

Self-knotted quickdraw and circular sling

Tape widths

The tapes used for making slings are between 15 and 25 mm wide. Narrow tapes with the same breaking strain as broad ones are preferable, particularly with modern light-weight karabiners, since loads are distributed more evenly between slings and karabiners, which increases the breaking strain. For this reason, some manufacturers also produce waisted slings.

Tape lengths

Quickdraws are used mainly in lengths of 10 to 15 cm and circular slings in lengths of 30 cm to 1.5 m (these figures refer to the loop length when fully extended, not the circumference, as given by some manufacturers). If you want to make slings yourself, you must include the material required for the knot (about 30 to 40 cm) when calculating the length of tape you need to buy.

Durability and care

Slings should not be used for more than three to four years, and should be handled as carefully as a rope.

Accessory cords

Function:
▶ make it possible to use natural rock features (principally threads) as anchors;
▶ can be used as slings with nuts;
▶ serve as prusik loops for self-rescue work;
▶ can be used as knotted cords (the traditional methods of protection in the Elbsandsteingebirge).

Materials

Accessory cords can be made of nylon, Kevlar, Dyneema or Spectra. The stretch property of accessory cord is considerably lower than that of climbing rope. However, the higher static breaking strength of Kevlar, Dyneema and Spectra is accompanied by other disadvantages. Kevlar is very susceptible to kinking (problematic with tight bends over edges) and Dyneema and Spectra have a lower melting point (145 °C) than nylon (250 °C).

Diameter and breaking strain

Accessory cords with diameters of between 4 and 9 mm are available. The breaking strain depends on the diameter. The relevant German standard stipulates a minimum breaking strain, calculated according to the following formula:

Breaking strain (kN) = diameter (mm) x diameter (mm) x 0.2

Example: 6 mm x 6 mm x 0.2 = 7.2 kN

Applications

Because of their higher breaking strain, you should use tape loops whenever possible. For this reason, accessory cords are not particularly widely used. If you want to connect an accessory cord to a tape loop (thread, nut loop, abseil loop, etc.), it is preferable to use a double fisherman's knot (p. 70). You can use a prusik loop (p. 71) to secure yourself when abseiling or climbing up a fixed rope. For this, you will need an accessory cord about 80 cm in length and 4 to 5 mm in diameter.

Durability

An accessory cord can be expected to last about two years. Prusik loops, however, last a considerably shorter time because of the constant rubbing on the rope.

Karabiners

Function:
▶ used to connect ropes, slings and anchors;
▶ for belaying.

Material

Lightweight karabiners made of aluminium alloys are the only ones suitable for freeclimbing, since steel karabiners are too heavy.

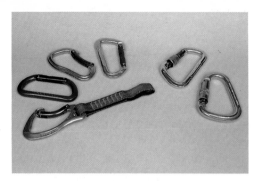

L. to r.: Karabiner with integral quickdraw, symmetrical D, asymmetrical D (bent gate), asymmetrical D (straight gate), screwgate fastening, Kwiklock fastening

Shapes

D-shaped and asymmetrical karabiners in various special shapes are now more popular than other designs because of their higher breaking strengths. Locking HMS karabiners (pear-shaped) are used only for belaying. When buying an HMS karabiner, be sure not to confuse it with other, similar-looking mountaineering karabiners.

Gates

In addition to straight gates, there are bent and angled gates. Bent gates make it easier to clip a rope in quickly. Angled gates remain in the open position and have to be snapped shut by hand. This is an advantage when clipping in a rope on anchors you can only just reach, but there is a risk that you will forget to close the karabiner again.

Locking karabiners

The gates on karabiners used for belaying, top-roping, abseiling and several other rope manoeuvres must be lockable in order to

prevent them opening inadvertently. There are several tried and tested systems on the market. Screwgate karabiners have a sleeve that must be pushed over the gate to lock it. Twistlock (Kwiklock), slide and bayonet fastenings lock automatically.

Tips on buying

The quality of a karabiner can be judged by the following criteria. The standard static breaking strain of 20kN is usually adequate. However, the breaking strain when the gate is open is crucial in determining the quality of a karabiner. It should be higher than the required standard of 6 kN, since the gate can easily be flicked open, and in the event of a fall a breaking strain of 6 kN is often too low. In order to achieve high breaking strains under such circumstances, a karabiner with an integral "quickdraw" tape loop has been developed. The gate opening should be as big as possible for clipping on to large rings, while the nose of the karabiner should be as thin as possible so that it can be clipped on to small pegs. A large cross-section is necessary if the rope is to form a relatively large angle at the karabiner. However, a karabiner should weigh as little as possible.

Durability

Karabiners hardly ever wear out. Only if they have been twisted out of shape by fall loads or have been dropped from a great height (beware of karabiners you may find at the bottom of a route) or if the gate or locking mechanism no longer function perfectly should they need replacing.

Nuts (chocks, wedges)

Function:
▶ placed in cracks or holes for protection and anchoring; quick to place and quick to remove.

Nuts are small pieces of metal made of aluminium alloys or brass threaded with wire cables or accessory cords.

Shapes

Apart from many often exotic-looking designs, the tapering wedge and irregular hexagonal shapes have become generally accepted. The faces of many tapering wedges (rocks, locknuts) are rounded off into half-moon shapes, which gives a more stable, three-point placement and thus increased holding power. Cutting notches into the faces (wall nuts) improves holding power in irregularly shaped cracks. The size of a wedge is normally indicated by giving it a number between one and nine. However, the actual sizes are not standardized and thus vary a great deal from manufacturer to manufacturer. Hexagonal nuts (hexentrics) are available in a wide range of different sizes.

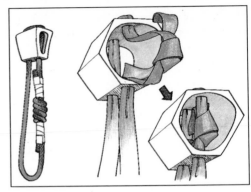
Self-knotted slings on nuts

From left to right: Brass nuts, nut remover, wall nuts with Spectra and wire cables, locknuts with Spectra and wire cables, hexentric with accessory cord

Wires and loops

Smaller wedges come with a wire cable attached to them, either threaded through or driven or soldered into a drill hole in the wedge. Larger nuts will accept accessory cords of nylon or, even better, Spectra (Dyneema). The relevant standard stipulates that retailers have to supply nuts with a wire or loop already attached. If the accessory cord on a nut has to be changed, choose a cord of the largest possible diameter that can be threaded through the drill hole. Then tie the cord into a loop with a double fisherman's knot (p. 70) and secure the ends with adhesive tape. With large hexcentrics with a drill hole more than 9 mm in diameter, use a tubular tape loop secured with a tape knot. With large nuts that are hollow inside, the knot can safely be stowed inside the wedge. The loop of cord should be between 20 and 30 cm in length. The strength of a nut depends largely on the cable or cord attached to it. The standard stipulates that each nut should bear a small star for each 5 kN of breaking strain. Small wedges should have at least one star, while larger ones should have a breaking strain of between 10 and 15 kN (two to three stars).

In each case, however, whether a wire cable, accessory cord or tubular tape loop is

attached, the edges of the drill hole must be smoothed off so that sharp edges cannot reduce the strength of the loop.

The advantage of a wire cable is that it makes the nut easier to place in narrow cracks. However, the stiffness of the cable means that rope movements are transmitted to the nut, which may be prised out of the crack as a result. Because they are more difficult to place, more flexible accessory cords can be used only with larger nuts.

Durability

The useful life of a nut depends on the wire or cord attached to it. If the wire or cord shows any visible signs of wear, the nut should be discarded or the cord replaced.

Removal tools

So-called "nutters" or "nut keys" can be used to improve the placement of or to remove nuts that have become tightly wedged in the depths of cracks.

Camming devices

Function:
▶ the only nut that works reasonably well in parallel or even outwardly flaring cracks; quick to place and to remove.

The ability of a camming device to expand in order to fit a crack perfectly relies on a more or less complicated spring-loaded mechanism. There are two basic types in common use.

Expanding cam devices

Expanding cam devices have one to four spring-loaded cams. They can be placed in parallel or slightly outwardly flaring cracks. When a load is applied, the pressure exerted by the cams on the rock increases in direct proportion to the load. The classic camming

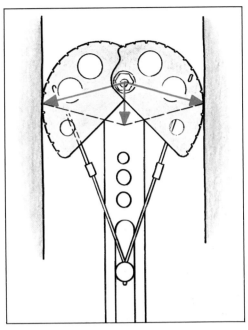

When a load is applied, the pressure exerted by the cams on the rock increases in direct proportion to the load

device is the "Friend", which consists of two opposed pairs of cams that move in opposite directions. However, in order to obtain a better three-point placement, devices with only three cams have now been developed (HB, Sphaero-T).

The strength of a camming device depends on its stem. A standard introduced in 1989 stipulates that, as with nuts, the stem of a camming device should bear a star for each 5 kN of breaking strain. Small devices should carry no fewer than two stars (i.e. have a minimum breaking strain of 10 kN), while large devices should have a minimum breaking strain of 15 kN (three stars). In order to avoid adverse leverage in horizon-

From left to right: Friend with rigid stem, Friend with flexible stem, Sphaero-T, slider

tal placements and transverse loads on the stem, rigid stems can be replaced with flexible ones. However, rigid stems are easier to place.

Sliders

A pair of wedges in opposition (slider) or a wedge with an adjustable metal cam can also be held in place in parallel cracks by a spring mechanism. Here again, the pressure exerted by the cam surfaces on the rock increases in proportion to the load applied. The factor that determines the breaking strain of such devices is the steel cable; the minimum rating should be 10 kN.

Durability

If the spring mechanism is damaged, if the stem or any other part of the device is twisted out of shape, if the tape loop is worn or if the cam teeth are showing signs of wear, then the camming device should be discarded or, in view of the cost of a new one, sent to the manufacturer or importer for repair.

Pitons (pegs)

Function:
▶ provide anchors that are to a large extent permanent and independent of direction of the load.

Unless you are making the first ascent of a route, or climbing an unfrequented or very remote one, you will find all the pitons considered necessary by the first person to climb the route. For this reason, this section on pitons will not go into great detail.

Shapes

Pitons, or pegs, come in a range of different shapes – angles (U- or V-shaped), bongs (large-angle pitons), Leepers (Z-shaped), knife blades and rurps (pegs with very thin blades) – and consist of a blade or wedge and a karabiner hole. They can be forged from hard steel (which is stronger, but suitable only for granite or basic rock) or soft steel (suitable for all types of rock). They are hammered into cracks and usually left in place until they rot.

Bolts are placed in dense rock. A hole is first drilled in the rock with a hammer and driver;

From left to right: Bolts with external expansion sleeves, rurp, Lost Arrow, angle, Leeper, knifeblade

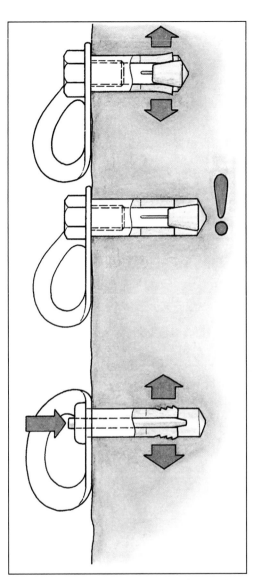

Expansion sleeve from the inside (top); drill hole is too deep, so the sleeve does not expand (middle); the external expansion sleeve works irrespective of the depth of the drill hole (bottom)

more recently, battery-powered drills have also come into use. The bolt is then fixed into the rock with quick-drying cement (Bühler, Eco Ancer) or special adhesives (AV-Haken) or wedged in by means of a sleeve that expands as the bolt is driven into the hole, which is then packed with sealant.

There are two kinds of expansion bolts. Old, but unfortunately still commonly used systems, in which the bolt is driven into an expansion sleeve previously placed in the hole, should be avoided: if the drill hole is too deep, the sleeve fails to expand and the bolt cannot be guaranteed to be mechanically sound. The relevant standard stipulates that such systems should no longer be commercially available — but there are still huge numbers of them attached to rock surfaces. On the other hand, bolts with external expansion sleeves can always be relied upon, since their expansion mechanism will function properly irrespective of drill-hole depth.

Figure-of-eight descenders

Function:
▶ controlled abseiling;
▶ securing a partner.

Shapes
As the name suggests, these descenders are shaped like a figure of eight. The multiple deflections of the rope as it passes through the figure of eight create such a high degree of friction that it is possible to slide down the rope without any great effort. It is important that the bends in the rope are as big as possible: if they are too small, the tendency of the rope to kink and to overheat increases considerably. Two figure-of-eight descenders that differ from the standard shape are the Anka Descender, which is considerably easier on the rope, and the angular figure of eight, through which the rope can pass by two different routes.

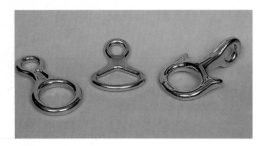

From left to right: Conventional figure-of-eight descender, angular figure of eight; Anka descender

Ascender, in this case a model without a handle

Durability

The operational life of a figure-of-eight descender is virtually unlimited. However, the useful life of a rope is shortened considerably by abseiling and severely affected by the type of descender used. Buying the wrong kind can be a false economy.

Ascenders

Function:
► to secure oneself to a fixed rope.

If you do not have a belay partner immediately to hand, you can secure yourself to a fixed rope with the aid of an ascender. An ascender can slide up the rope but locks when loaded. This can also be done with a prusik knot, although this method is not so comfortable.

Shapes

Ascenders come with or without a handle. An ascender without a handle is adequate for freeclimbing. Just make sure there is a hole at the front and back to clip on a karabiner and that the locking mechanism on the clamping lever is in place.

Chalk (carbonate of magnesium)

Function:
► to soak up finger and hand sweat.

White chalk is bought in blocks and crushed to a powder for use. Gymnasts and weightlifters have been using it for a long time in order to improve their grip. In hot weather and on difficult climbs, the use of chalk undoubtedly increases performance, since dry hands slip considerably less in holds than hands that are damp with sweat.

A variety of chalkbags to suit every taste, and a block of chalk

Chalkbag

Free climbers carry powdered chalk in a cloth bag attached to the back of their harness. These bags are available in bright colours and a variety of different sizes. The bag should have a pile lining, a stiffened edge at the top to keep it open and a flap or drawcord to prevent chalk spilling in transit. The material used to make the bag should be dustproof.

Application

By applying chalk and then dusting it off again, hands and fingers can be dried of sweat. Put your fingers in the chalkbag up to your palm and rub them against the pile lining or directly in the chalk. Remove any surplus chalk by wiping your hand on the edge of the bag, or blowing or shaking it off. This procedure is called chalking, and should be repeated whenever you feel your fingers are too sweaty. This is how those impressive photos materialise, in which a climber is rummaging around casually in his chalkbag with one hand while clinging on to an overhang with the other. With many climbers, however, repeated use of the chalk is either a reflection of their nervousness or simply an unconscious habit which wastes a lot more energy than is actually necessary.

Environmental considerations

The subject of chalk and its environmental impact often gives rise to passionate debate among more conservative contemporaries but among aficionados it is a highly symbolic item of equipment. However that may be, chalk has been demonstrated not to cause any environmental damage, although it does deface the rock; manufacturers have responded to this concern by producing

Isabelle Patissier shakes chalk from her hand

coloured chalk to suit a variety of different rock colours.

Only in sandstone and granite regions can chalk cause any real damage, as it blocks the pores in the rock. It is for this reason that chalk has been banned in some sandstone regions, or at least climbers are expected to clean a route after they have climbed it. In these areas, resin is sometimes used instead of chalk.

Despite its environmentally friendly reputation, chalk should still be used sensibly and on cool days and on easy routes it is not usually necessary at all. Excessive use of chalk on rocks and on descent and approach rock merely provokes criticism. Whether or not you feel yourself to be in the right, this is not exactly beneficial for the sport as a whole.

Clothing

Clothing can be left almost entirely to individual imagination and taste. The only real restrictions are that it needs to be flexible enough to allow great freedom of movement and appropriate to the weather conditions you expect to encounter. So particular care and attention should be given to the choice of clothing for alpine routes. As for the rest, however, it remains up to each individual to decide how far he or she chooses to pursue fashion trends, to demonstrate opportunism or to resist consumerist temptation by making do with clothes already available.

Clothing is entirely a matter for individual imagination and taste

Basic gear for the practice crag

Basic gear for practice crags

- a pair of high-friction climbing shoes;
- a sit and chest harness;
- a tubular sling about 1.8 m in length to link the sit and chest harness;
- a helmet;
- a locking HMS karabiner;
- a locking karabiner;
- a 1.2 m loop for a triangular sling configuration;
- a figure-of-eight descender.

In addition, each rope team will require:
- one single or two double ropes;
- ten quickdraws (about 10 cm long) each with two standard karabiners;
- a 30 cm sling;
- a 60 cm sling.

Nothing more should usually be necessary on well-developed, not too long routes on practice crags. Nevertheless, you should enquire about the protection required in each particular case. For routes that are protected by nuts, a set of nuts is recommended:
- five biconical nuts (wallnuts, rocks), sizes 1, 3, 5, 7 and 9;
- three hexentrics, sizes 5, 7 and 9.

Camming devices, such as Friends, should not be used until you have some climbing experience.

This list is for guidance only, and is intended to ensure that you are not over- or underequipped, or wrongly equipped out of sheer inexperience. However, the gear you carry must be adapted to the characteristics of each particular area. Over time, a climber will assemble a rack to suit her own experience and the habits she has developed.

Climbing Techniques

Nowhere in the world are there two identical climbing routes, and even on artificial climbing walls a slight change in the architecture and size of foot and handholds or in the distances between them can make it necessary to adopt completely different postures and different methods of preserving balance and strength giving rise to alternative routes. The range of climbing positions and routes is as diverse as the range of natural or artificial rock structures that can be climbed. This is why there are no established techniques, but merely basic forms of a range of techniques that have to be adapted to each individual situation. Nor is any one technique necessarily the only method of getting over a particular hurdle, since any individual section of a route can often be climbed in entirely different ways.

Basic techniques

Climbing means controlling and stabilizing the body's centre of gravity above a narrow base and then moving on from there up the rock face, which hardly makes the task an easy one. The actions of moving upwards and catching one's balance again must be performed as economically as possible, that is with the least possible expenditure of energy required for a particular move. Since human endurance is limited, using energy efficiently is the only way of climbing fluently and untiringly, not only on difficult climbs but on easier ones as well. There is a close relationship between strength and technique so that the better the technique, the lesser the strength required to climb. Or in other words, the best climber is the one who completes the climb with the least expenditure of energy. An experienced climber conserves his or her energy and therefore tires more slowly. Particular attention should be paid to this fact in training. General fitness training intended to improve strength, stamina and agility should play a subordinate, supporting role, with the practice of climbing techniques taking priority.

Handwork

In general terms, there are four basic kinds of grip in freeclimbing.

Palm hold

With the palm hold, the weight of the climber's body is supported on the rock with the palms of the hand turned outwards or inwards. Such a hold does not normally require a particularly prominent stow. The palm hold is the most economical technique, and all too frequently one can see climbers making the mistake of pulling themselves up with both hands rather than using the palm hold, which means they are wasting energy.

Flat holds

With flat holds, the fingers are placed on holds such as more or less horizontal ledges, hollows and edges. The aim is to bring as many fingers as possible into contact with the rock and to adjust the shape of the hand as closely as possible to that of the hold.

Moulding the shape of the hand in this way to the structure of the rock ensures maximum transference of energy.

When learning and practising flat holds, you should get used right from the beginning to keeping the ends of the fingers as straight as possible in the hold rather than curling them up. Otherwise the constant shearing stress in the finger joints can lead to arthritis, which is the commonest climbing injury caused by repetitive stress. And in any case, the straighter the fingers are, the less strength is required to hold them in position. Particularly in training, you should try as hard as possible to avoid curling the fingers up.

However, if small ledges cannot be climbed with straight fingers, you will have to curl them up. The stress absorbed by the knuckles when the fingers are bent sharply at the first knuckle is more painful on the fingertips. However, this technique is actually less stressful on the finger joints than bending the fingers at the second knuckle. The thumb can sometimes be wrapped over the index finger for support.

1   2   3   4

Picture 1: Palm hold
Picture 2: Flat hold with fingers as straight as possible – this method avoids shearing stress in the finger joints

Picture 3: Flat hold with fingers curled up. The thumb is wrapped over the index finger for support
Picture 4: Flat hold with fingers bent sharply at the first knuckle

Holding on with a finger crimp

In holes and on very narrow ledges, you will have to grip with individual fingers. It is sometimes possible to stack the other fingers on top of each other for support. However, the risk of injury is very high, since the entire load is concentrated on just one or two joints, and in the event of a fall, the finger can remain jammed in the hole, which can cause serious injuries to ligaments and tendons.

Undercuts and sidepulls (layaways)

With this technique, the direction of pull is different. An undercut functions through the counter-pressure exerted by the feet and legs. With a sidepull, you lean away from the hold, with the hands and feet working in opposition.

In holes in the rock, you have to hold on with individual fingers. This is a two-finger pocket

An undercut is held by counter-pressure exerted by the legs

A sidepull is held by shifting the weight of the body as you lean away from the hold

46

Manfred Eichhorn clinging on to a one-finger pocket on the "Ghettoblaster" (X) route on the Rabenfels

47

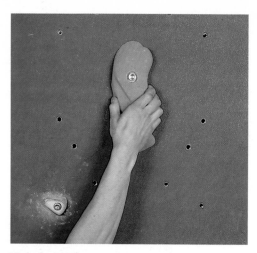

The pinch grip

The pinch grip

With knobs, ribs or other protuberances, use the counter-pressure exerted by the thumb to form a pincer. Once again, you should try to keep the fingers as straight as possible rather then curling them up.

In order to ensure an economical climbing style, it is important to change grip as often as possible. Since each kind of hold brings only certain muscles or groups of muscles into play, frequent switches of hold give the muscles not being used a chance to recover. You should even make every effort to practise the so-called soft grip, i.e. the one requiring the least expenditure of energy.

Footwork

The strongest muscles are those in the legs. For this reason alone, it is important that the legs bear as much of the weight of the body as possible, in order to take the strain off the arm muscles.

Generally, you will want to place as much of the sole of the foot as possible over the surface area of the foothold. You will normally step on to the foothold using the area of the sole beneath the big toe. As you do so, your ankle should be held neither too high nor too low. Your weight should be correctly balanced over your feet in order to minimize the risk of sliding. You can step on to small ledges with the inner ball of the foot, while with sidepulls and traverses the outer ball can also come into play.

Smear holds are footholds that are so sloping the foot only stays in place by friction. The foot should be held as vertically as possible as it is placed carefully on the hold. The heel should be held considerably lower than with normal holds. The quality of a smear hold is determined not by the size of the area of contact between sole and rock, as is often wrongly supposed, but rather by pushing down with the toes with the right amount of force and in the right direction in order to hold the smear. These factors combine automatically to produce the appropriate area of contact.

When you have found a good foothold for a particular move, you will jeopardize your secure position by twisting your feet or teetering about. On sandstone or on very weathered rock, such movements may even cause dislodged grains of rock to form clumps that act almost like ball bearings, reducing the friction that holds the foot in place. You must make sure that the sole of your foot is free of grains of rock by wiping it on the other leg before placing it in another foothold. There is

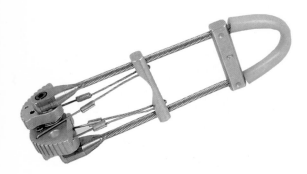

Stepping on to a hold with the heel held too high

Stepping on to a hold with the heel held too low

Stepping on to a hold with the heel held in the correct position

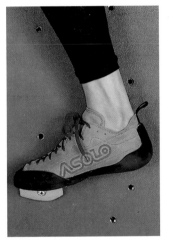

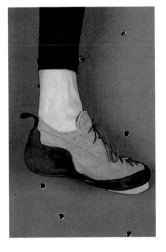

Stepping on to a hold with the inner ball of the foot

Stepping on to a hold with the outer ball of the foot

Stepping on to a smear hold – the heel is held low

one exception that proves the rule: on firm chalk or granite, twisting the ball of the foot before stepping on to a hold actually increases the friction by roughening up the soles of the shoes. Contrary to previous schools of thought, it is now considered a good idea to use your knees when it is sensible to do so, for example when climbing large ledges. This is a useful addition to the repertoire of moves.

Basic position

The basic body position is the one that ensures stability on the rock face, the one that every climber should strive for after completing a move. The body's centre of gravity should be directly over the base (i.e. the connecting line between the two footholds). Logically, on low-angle faces the

The basic climbing position

body should not be too close to the face, while on steep slopes it should not be positioned too far away from the rock. Otherwise, the arms would have to bear more body weight than necessary. In the basic stable position, the weight of the body is borne mainly by the legs, which should also be spread slightly for sideways stability. A widely held but incorrect view has it that straightening joints completely (e.g. by stretching the legs to their fullest extent) is disadvantageous, since maximum muscle power can be applied only in the bent position. However, this theory, well known in sports physiology, also states that, with the limbs in a bent position, energy has constantly to be expended. Thus it is perfectly permissible to extend the limbs fully in order to save energy.

However, you should avoid overextending the whole body, since this will bring it too close to the rock. The body's centre of gravity will no longer be directly over the support area, the load on footholds and handholds will be wrongly distributed, and your field of vision will be obstructed because your face will be too close to the rock.

Moving on rock

The technique for moving up a rock face is based on three important basic rules:
1. The three-point rule: three points of the body (e.g. two hands and one foot) maintain contact with the rock while the fourth limb (in this case, the other foot) is being moved. In this way, the body remains in a stable position as a move is made, since simultaneously stretching up with the hand and stepping on to a new foothold can very easily lead to a loss of balance.
2. Static-reversible climbing: each move must be reversible if, for example, a handhold does not live up to expectations. On more difficult routes, however, the considerably riskier dynamic-irreversible climbing style is often necessary (p. 65).
3. The legs should do most of the work involved in propelling your mass upwards, with the hands being used essentially only for steadying purposes. Of course this can be achieved consistently only on low-angle slopes in the lower grades of technical difficulty. Nevertheless, efficient use of the legs can save an enormous amount of strain on the arms, even on vertical and overhanging routes.

In theory, then, these three basic rules make the technique involved in moving on rock sound pretty commonplace: starting from the basic position, it is simply a matter of moving a foot or a hand higher up the rock face. However, in order to maintain your balance as you move up the rock, you should select footholds and handholds that are not too far apart from each other; if the distances between them are too great, any forward movement will be jerky and require greater energy expenditure. It is better to select a less favourable hold that is closer to you and allows you to move fluidly while retaining your balance than to heave yourself awkwardly over larger distances. When the distance between holds is large (or, in tricky

Climbing technique

The finer points of climbing technique

Shifting the centre of gravity

The most important element of climbing technique is being able to shift the centre of gravity correctly while moving. There are a few sequences of movements that can frequently be employed to good advantage when trying to keep your weight directly over your feet.

Every climber very quickly realizes that his or her knees are in the way on steep routes. The normal forwards and upwards movement of the knee would force the body away from the wall. As a result, the body's centre of gravity would no longer be directly over the base, and the hands would have to bear a lot of the weight unnecessarily. In order to bring the body closer to the rock face, the knees have to be turned away to the side, so as to move up the rock, so as you bring your foot up the knee is bent and turned away to the side. Before moving the second foot upwards, shift your weight on to the first foot and then bring the second foot up with the knee turned to the side in the same way. This will bring you into the so-called "frog position". Incidentally, this is a very comfortable position to maintain with outstretched arms. The body is then propelled upwards by pushing simultaneously with both legs.

This principle of shifting the body's centre of gravity can also be used to negotiate sections of a route on which you cannot get into the frog position with the knees flexed as far as possible. However, it is important that you shift your weight on to the other leg before moving on. In doing so, you should always twist your knee to one side and keep your body close to the rock face.

positions, even when the distance is small), it may be that the foot that is being moved upwards will actually be required to maintain balance. This will become evident if the foot scrapes awkwardly over the rock. This phenomenon is known as "moving under pressure". It should be avoided as far as possible, as should snatching for handholds, which has the same causes.

The danger as well as the attraction of climbing lie in the fact that, depending on the difficulty of the climb, footholds and handholds are seldom to be found where they are required in order to maintain the correct basic position and to allow movement up the rock.

① Shifting the centre of gravity …

③ into the frog position …

② over the next foothold …

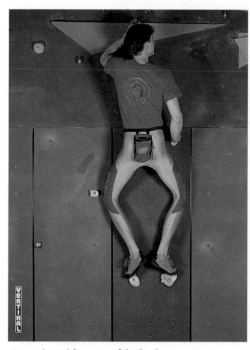

④ and pushing up with the legs

Isabelle Patissier in the frog position

Bending the body to climb an overhang

In this way, your centre of gravity will always be over one or other of your feet. Changing the type of hold can often be a very economical way of shifting your balance in this way. By bracing yourself on the rock or using sidepulls (a hand hold that needs to be held with a horizontal pull), it is often amazingly easy to shift the centre of gravity. Bracing the body also takes some of the strain away from the arms.

Climbing overhangs
You should climb overhangs with straight arms whenever possible, since the arms tire much more quickly when bent. Here, too, it is sensible in most situations to keep the centre of gravity close to the rock face. This can be achieved by bending the body, thus shifting weight from the hands to the feet.
Another method of shifting the centre of gravity closer to the rock face is to twist the body. With this method, use the outer balls of your feet to step on to footholds and underclings to steady yourself.

Twisting the body to climb an overhang

Climbing traverses

Traverses can usually be climbed fluently by leap-frogging the legs, one over the other, twisting the body and making use of sidepulls. In this way, you can save yourself a change of foothold.

③ **making use of sidepulls ...**

① **Climbing a traverse ...**

② **by leap-frogging the legs, twisting the body ...**

④ **and shifting the weight of the body from one foot to the other ...**

⑤ **saves the climber a change of foothold**

Swinging out (the "barn door" effect)

There are situations on vertical or overhanging sections in which the climber swings outwards while changing hold. In such circumstances, he or she rotates around the foot-handhold axis, while the other foot, hitherto resting securely on a hold, swings away

... The foot swings ...

Twisting around the (oblique) foot-handhold axis ...

... away from the wall

from the rock face. The same phenomenon occurs with a door that is hung on the slant, hence the term "barn door" effect. There are several ways of dealing with this situation. For example, you can let your foot swing back in towards the rock and then reach for the hold again. This infringes the three-point rule, but of course exceptions prove the rule. A second option is to leap-frog the legs, one over the other, which has the effect of supporting the swinging motion on the rock. You can also straighten the crooked foot-handhold axis by a change of foothold.

Smearing (W. Gullich, K. Albert)

Smearing

Smearing is a foot technique used on slabs (flat, apparently featureless pieces of rock), in which virtually the whole of the body's weight is borne by the feet. The hands are used solely for support and to maintain balance.

With this technique, it is especially important to keep the centre of gravity directly above the base. In contrast to the position adopted when climbing vertical faces or overhangs, you should hold your body away from the rock in order to maximize the downward pressure exerted by the feet. For optimal transmission of pressure to the rock, the heels are dropped down low. Short distances between footholds and calm, well-balanced moves are characteristic of this technique. The legs should not be spread too far apart, since all unnecessary swaying to and fro should be avoided as you move.

Leap-frogging the legs straightens the axis

A change of foothold straightens the axis

Laybacking

This extremely strenuous technique relies on the hands and feet working in opposition. Hands, feet and the body's centre of gravity, leaning off to one side, create pressure and counter-pressure. The technique is used to climb vertical ribs of rock or cracks with an area of footholds running parallel to them. High friction means that the feet can find footholds even on a smooth, vertical wall. The friction is all the greater the further to one side you shift your centre of gravity by bringing your arms and legs as close together as possible. Unfortunately, this makes the whole manoeuvre even more strenuous and requires extraordinary body strength.

In every phase of the manoeuvre, the arms should remain as straight as possible. Forward movement, grabbing the next handhold and stepping on to the next foothold take place by leap-frogging arms and legs one over the other or, if that is not possible, by shuffling the lower arm or leg up to the top limb. Either way, you will soon be sweating.

Laybacking can also be used in other situations, for example when using side holds on traverses.

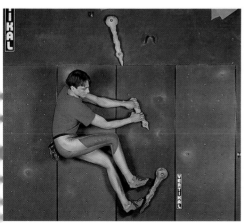

Laybacking

Crack-climbing skills

Crack-climbing is one of the most painful enterprises in climbing. Nevertheless, with time and technique acquired through experience, it is possible to acquire such a taste for it that many crack fetishists get completely carried away, preferring "jamming" to good handholds. Cracks come in a huge range of widths. The variety of techniques used to climb them is correspondingly extensive; the most important ones will be outlined here.

Finger cracks
If the crack is just wide enough to get your fingers in, jam them in up to the middle joint with the thumbs pointing down. With the wrist bent and the arm pulling down, the fingers become locked in the crack.

Hand cracks
With a hand crack, place the hand inside the crack with the thumb pointing up and then wedge the thumb into the palm. You can now jam your feet into the crack by turning the soles inwards as if you were trying to stand on the outer edge of your shoes, placing the foot inside the crack and twisting it back into the horizontal position. In order to free your foot, you will have to twist it back out again in the same way. For this reason, small steps are recommended.

Fist jamming
The hand is placed horizontally inside the crack and then clenched into a fist.

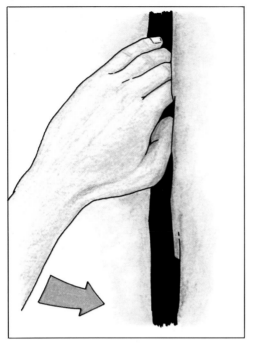

Finger crack

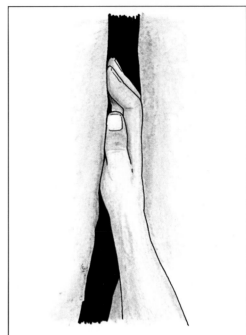

Hand crack

Crack-climbing demonstrated by Stefan Glowacz, London Wall, E5, 6a. Millstone Edge

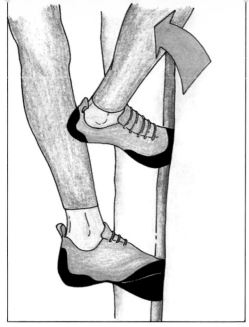

Jamming the feet into a hand crack

Off-width cracks

With off-width cracks, jam one half of the body into the crack. The arm inside the crack is bent and presses the shoulder and upper arm against the rock; the other arm presses against the edge of the crack from the outside. The leg inside the crack is wedged in place by counter-pressure from the knee and foot; the outer foot is jammed against the edge of the crack. The wider the crack, the further inside the body is jammed. The boundaries between off-width techniques and stemming are fluid, as between cracks and chimneys.

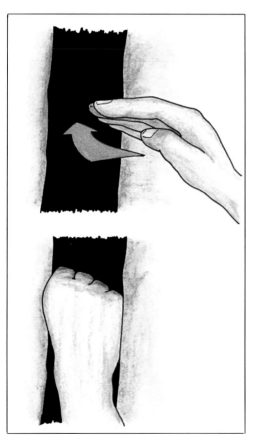

Fist jamming

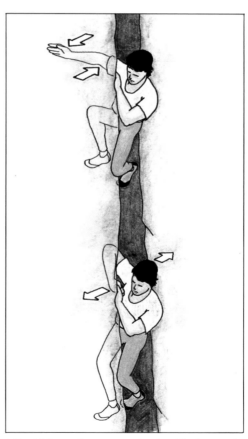

Off-width cracks: narrow (top), wide (bottom)

Stemming or bridging

The technique of stemming is based on the counter-pressure principle and is used in chimneys, which are very wide cracks. The hands and/or feet are pressed against one side of the chimney, while the back is braced against the other side. This technique can be used so long as the chimney is no wider than your legs are long.

In narrow chimneys, use your arms to press the upper half of your body against the opposite side of the chimney and then pull the legs up as far as you can. Then use counter-pressure from the feet and knees to jam the legs and push the upper body upwards. If the chimney becomes wider, use both legs to wedge the upper body against the opposite wall. Then place the hands, palms outwards, on the opposite wall at the level of the buttocks and push the upper body away from

Stemming in a narrow chimney

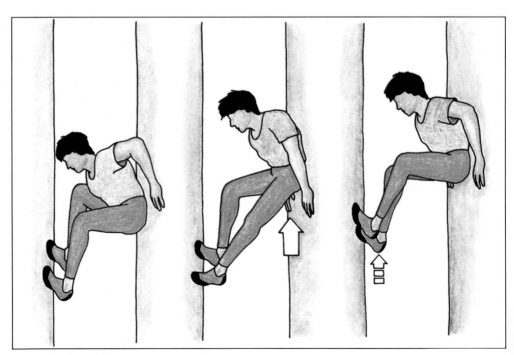

Stemming in a chimney of normal width

Bridging a wide chimney

the wall in an upwards direction. You can also place one foot on this side of the chimney in order to help work the body upwards. Then use both feet to wedge your back again against the opposite side of the chimney and bridge your way up in small steps.

If the chimney opens up further, a change of technique is required. You will have to "bridge" the chimney, using one hand and one foot on each wall. Using this technique, you will often find yourself having to spread your legs very wide and hoping that the chimney does not get any wider as you work your way towards your goal by alternately moving one foot or hand upwards.

Edi Becker bridging a wide chimney

The technique for climbing a corner crack (dihedral)

Climbing corner cracks (dihedrals)

The technique for climbing inside corners (dihedrals) is very similar to bridging or stemming. By straddling corners or grooves, the body's centre of gravity is kept directly over its base. Ideally, the whole of the body's weight should be borne by the feet, thus taking all the strain off the hands. If the right foot is to be moved next, for example, drop your right hand down lower than the left and push on it for support so that the right foot can be taken off and moved up.

Climbing a corner crack – the view from below

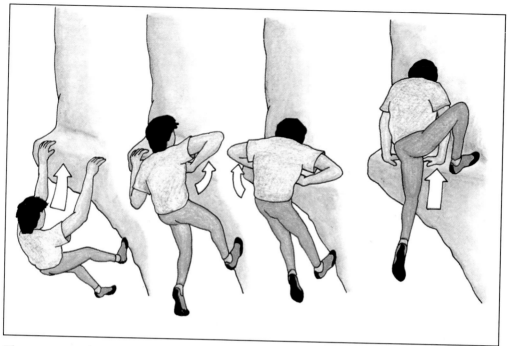

The sequence of moves involved in an overhanging mantle

Special climbing techniques

Mantling

Quite often, you will find yourself having to climb a ledge above which there are no holds to be seen. Thus the only visible means of support is the lip or edge of the ledge itself. And if there are only scant footholds below, then things can get really strenuous.

In order to surmount such a rock feature, place both hands on the ledge and hoist yourself up, shifting the body's centre of gravity as high up as you can. The next step is to cock both arms on the ledge, either simultaneously or one after the other. To do this, turn your arms inwards, with the fingertips pointing in towards the body. Finally, press up off the ledge and step up into the standing position. Mantling comes very close to dynamic climbing, since the upward impetus of the body is used to move the arms into the cocked position.

An expert mantling. Manfred Eichhorn on the climbing wall in Nuremberg

Foot hook (Matthias Pausch)

Foot hooks

With a foot hook, the heel or top of the foot is hooked over or jammed into a hold above the body's centre of gravity. Along with many other imaginative climbing manoeuvres, the foot hook is used mainly on overhangs and roofs. In order to surmount overhangs, hook your heel on to the overhang before pulling yourself up to reach the hold. In this way, you take the strain off your arms.

On horizontal roofs, a foot hook can prevent a climber from swinging out (the so-called "barn door" effect). In this case, the top of the foot is hooked into a suitable rock feature. However, foot hooks are not by themselves the complete answer to the problem of climbing a roof. In order to avoid pendulum swings, and the usually inevitable slipping off holds that follows, body tension is more necessary than in any other climbing manoeuvre.

Dynamic climbing

Dynamic moves constitute the most difficult and risky technique in freeclimbing, and no climber should even think of using "dynamos" until so-called static moves have been practised so thoroughly that they have become second nature and can be coordinated down to the last detail. Dynamic moves are based on a simple principle, but the patterns of movement, in contrast, are very complex.

It is impossible in many situations to reach the next hold in the static, reversible style. This may be because the hold being used is too small to support the climber's weight as he moves to the next hold. If one hand were to let go of the second hold in order to clasp another one, the climber would fall. Another reason is the fact that, if the distance between holds is very great, the body must be straightened up, which changes the direction of pull on the lower hold, to the point where it may no longer even be secure. And sometimes, the next hold is simply too far away to be grabbed. A mistake frequently made in such situations is to try to snatch at the hold without gaining any momentum. This merely guarantees that you will fall backwards off the rock as soon as one hand lets go of its grip.

With dynamic moves, on the other hand, you vault off a hold and are propelled upwards to another. You achieve this by crouching down

Dynamic climbing

as far as possible in the climbing position and then pulling explosively from the arms, gaining added propulsion from the feet as they kick off their holds. At the apex of the leap, the so-called "dead point", there is a brief moment of weightlessness that you can take advantage of to grab the hold. All the power of the trunk and arms is required to halt the downward movement of the body that sets in immediately afterwards.

Coordinating the momentum and direction of the entire move, which depends on the interplay of various groups of muscles, requires a highly developed sense of movement. And if the move fails, a fall is often unavoidable. For this reason, dynamic climbing is often called the "irreversible climbing style", meaning that, once you are committed, there is no going back. So a dynamo should not be undertaken half-heartedly. Once you have decided to "throw" a dynamic move, it must be executed in precisely the right sequence and without any hesitation.

There is a very high risk of injury to the fingers with this technique, since if an attempted dynamo fails, a large part of the body's weight is taken for a critical moment by the grasping fingers.

Downclimbing

In order to get off a crag after successfully completing a route, you can downclimb on low-angle terrain with your back towards the rock face. Use the hands for support and keep the upper part of the body bent well forward. Climb down on your feet until your arms are bent, then change your handholds. On steeper terrain, climb down with your face to the wall. As you do so, try to select handholds that are as low as possible; the sequence of movements is the reverse of that used during the ascent.

A controlled fall

Falling

There are basically two ways of falling: controlled and uncontrolled. Controlled falls are unavoidable in modern freeclimbing if you are continuously seeking to push your personal performance to the limits in order to improve it. If you are to fall in a controlled manner, several preconditions must be met:

▶ the terrain must be suitable for falling (i.e. it should be vertical or overhanging) so there is no risk of colliding with the rock as you fall;

▶ the falling distance must be short;

▶ the protection must be totally reliable (p. 87);

▶ the belay station must be absolutely safe and the belayer experienced.

If you cannot be 100 per cent certain of all these points, the possibility of a fall involves incalculable risks and should be avoided at all costs. Under such circumstances, it is far preferable to climb back to the last reliable belay station than to carry on regardless.

You must be able to prepare yourself for a controlled fall. Warn your belay partner first by yelling out, then launch yourself deliberately into the air. You must jump far enough away from the rock to minimize the risk of hitting it as you fall, but not so far away that the inevitable swing is so great that any collision with the rock would be unnecessarily dangerous. On vertical or overhanging climbs, you generally do not need to launch yourself with any great power. As you fall, you should keep yourself in the upright position, facing the rock. Keep your legs bent and spread apart and your back rounded. Never be tempted to grab hold of the rope coming from your belay partner! Either place your hands on the rope knot on your sit harness or stretch them out in front of you.

Since it is virtually impossible to correct or adjust your body position as you fall, the most important thing in a controlled fall is to launch yourself correctly. If this proves impossible, you will be swung against the rock. Whenever possible, you should absorb the impact of any such collision with just your feet.

In the event of a pendulum fall (i.e. if you lose contact with the rock at a point to one side of the last belay station), you would, if you jumped directly backwards, slam into the wall and then get dragged further along the rock in an uncontrolled way. In this case, you should jump off the rock in the direction of the last belay station.

In order to practise your falling technique, you should make your way gradually and cautiously − and with 100 per cent protection − to heights from which a fall may reasonably be made.

Uncontrolled falls normally occur when something unforeseen happens, for example if you slide off a hold or part of your protection fails. In such cases, rapid application of the falling technique you have learnt can often help you avoid the worst conse-

quences. This is why it is always important for every climber to practise his or her falling technique.

If a planned fall goes wrong and you lose control, the cause is usually either an inadequate falling technique or a false assessment of the situation. In both cases, the causes must be analysed in order to prevent the mistake occurring again.

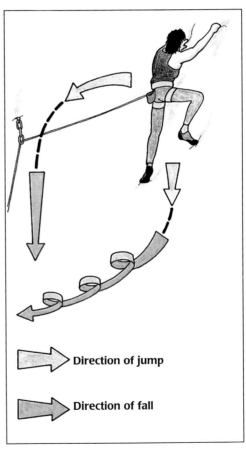

Direction of jump

Direction of fall

Avoiding a pendulum fall by jumping off in the direction of the intermediate protection

Protection Techniques

To many people, learning protection techniques seems to be the boring bit of freeclimbing.

Nevertheless, they are of fundamental importance, since the very life of a climber depends on secure protection. Moreover, the enormous improvement in performance in free climbing has come about only because the risk of injury – at least on practice crags – has been minimized by improved protection equipment and techniques. Nevertheless, tragic accidents continue to happen, and most are attributable to inadequate knowledge or careless implementation of protection techniques. Thus it is utterly vital for freeclimbers to familiarize themselves with this relatively untechnical aspect of the sport. The correct implementation of protection techniques always starts with the question "what would happen if …".

Beginners and advanced climbers alike must pay due attention to protection. The former often find themselves in situations beyond their technical capacities, while the latter tend to be neglectful.

Knots

Climbers simply cannot get by without knots. So it is appropriate at this point to outline the most important of the vast range of possible knots. You should be able to tie these knots perfectly, without looking, with just your left hand. As you do so, make sure that the strands of rope are lying correctly and that they are not excessively twisted inside the knot; if they are, the additional shearing forces will reduce the strength of the knot. Make sure you leave a reasonable amount of rope at either end of the knot: at least ten times the diameter of the rope (with an 11 mm rope, therefore, there should be at least 11 cm of rope spare at either end).

Overhand knot
- to knot double ropes together

Tape knot
- to form tape slings

Figure-of-eight
- to join the climbing rope to the harness

Bowline
- an alternative tie-in knot for connecting the climbing rope to the harness

Double fisherman's knot
- to join accessory cords

Clove hitch
- to secure the belayer to a karabiner attached to an anchor

Munter or Italian hitch (HMS)
- for belaying

Lark's foot
- to attach a sling to a tree or other anchor

Prusik knot
- to secure oneself to the rope when abseiling
- to secure oneself to a rope in order to ascend it

Slip knot
- to keep a Munter hitch in place under strain (after a fall)

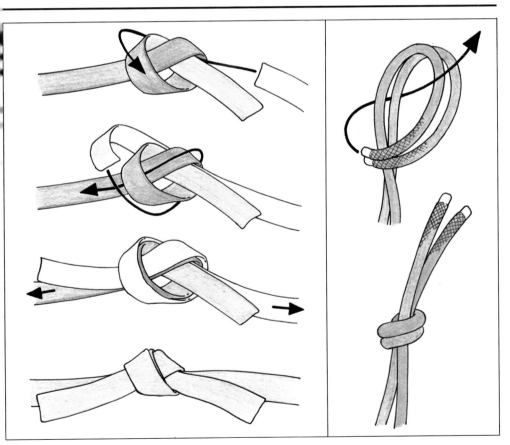

Tape knot (left), overhand knot (right)

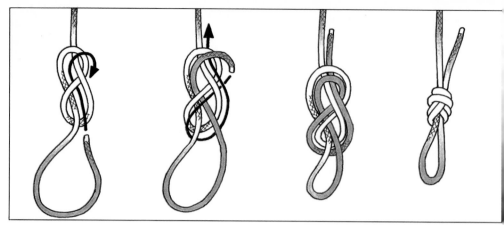

Figure-of-eight follow-through

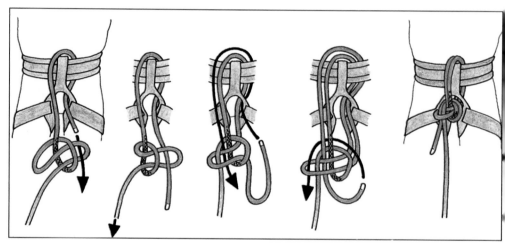

Bowline

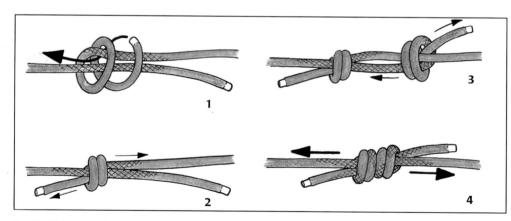

Double fisherman's knot

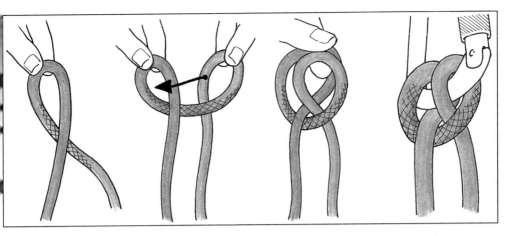

Clove hitch

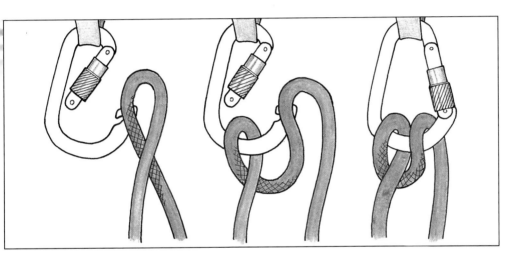

Munter or Italian hitch

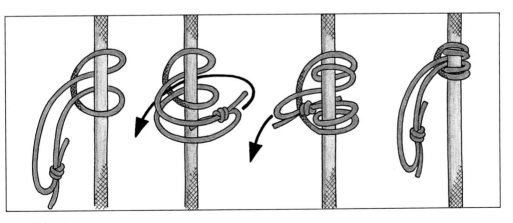

Prusik knot

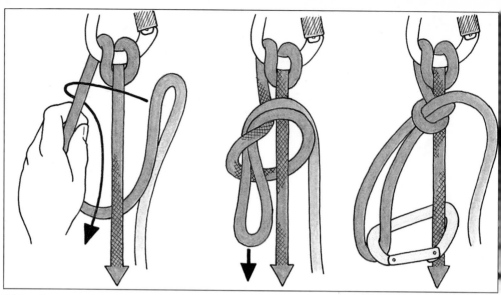

Slipknots

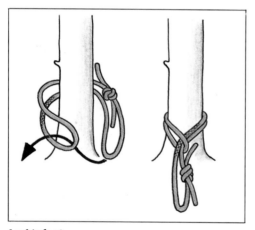

Lark's foot

Tie-in methods

Before you can really get under way, you have to connect your harness to the rope. If you are using a combined sit and chest harness, the two parts have to be joined by the figure-of-eight tape method. For this, you will require a piece of tubular tape about 1.8 m in length.

You should check that the connecting tape is correctly positioned by dangling in it and noting the relative proportions that best suit you. The tape is properly positioned when the sit harness is bearing the main load, the chest harness is not cutting into the flesh or constricting movement and the tie-in point is located immediately in front of the breast-bone when the harness is loaded.

This method of connecting the two parts of the harness has several advantages over other methods. The tie-in point is located above the body's centre of gravity, which means that a good body position can be maintained during falls. You cannot topple over backwards, and yet the upper part of the body has sufficient freedom of movement to lean backwards if necessary, for example when abseiling. Also, the sit and chest harnesses remain connected if you untie yourself from the rope, which is particularly advantageous when abseiling.

The rope is attached to the tie-in point using a figure-of-eight follow-through or a bowline. You must make sure that the free end of the

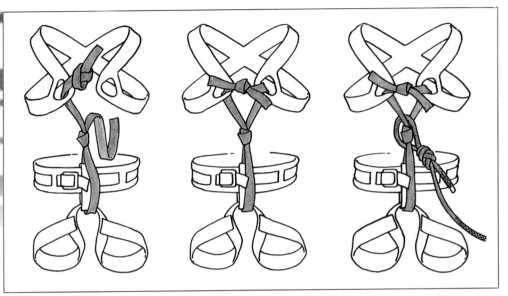

Tying-in with the figure-of-eight tape method

rope is long enough – at least 10 to 15 cm is necessary. If you are just using a sit harness, attach the rope to the tie-in loop or wrap it round the waist belt and through the loop connecting the waist belt and leg loops.

The bowline has the advantage of being easier to untie after a fall than a figure-of-eight but is somewhat more complicated to tie. The figure-of-eight follow-through is recommended for beginners, therefore. If the design of a particular harness makes it impossible to use the method described above, you will have to consult the instructions for use and rely on the manufacturer's knowledge and expertise.

Anchors

The climber is now attached to the rope, but that alone is of little use: if a fall is to be prevented, he or she must also be attached to the rock. There are several kinds of anchor, both natural and artificial.

Pitons (pegs)

On practice crags, you will mainly find expansion bolts, which have long been regarded as secure anchors, and doubtless will continue to be in the future. However, only properly placed bolts can be considered safe in the long term, and this is impossible to detect by visual inspection. However, as a rule, bolts with external expansion sleeves or those that

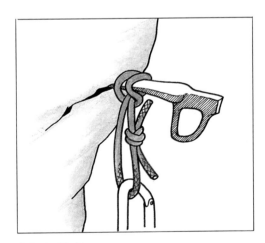

A tied-off piton

73

have been cemented or glued into position can usually be relied upon.

Ordinary pitons are particularly widely used in alpine regions although it is very difficult to judge whether or not they are safe as they have often been in the rock for decades, gently rusting away. They may not move even with a sharp tug, but their strength when fully loaded is not so easy to check. So a certain degree of cautious scepticism is therefore in order. Really important anchors, such as at the belay station, must also be secured with other protection devices (nuts, etc.).

If a peg is not fully driven into the rock, it must be tied off with an accessory cord or a tubular loop (as shown on p. 73). In this way, any load will not exert a large leverage force on the eye.

Nuts (chocks, wedges)

Nuts are placed in gradually narrowing cracks and, if well placed, make very reliable anchors. When placing a nut, you must take account of the following points:

► the rock around the placement must be absolutely sound. A sure indication of a brittle rock structure is the dull sound it emits when struck;

► the rock structures around the nut must be sufficiently dense to withstand the very high pressures generated when the nut is placed under load as slight irregularities in the crack may be blasted away under pressure and the nut may lift out;

► nuts usually wedge in one direction only and so they must be placed in such a way that when pulled in the anticipated

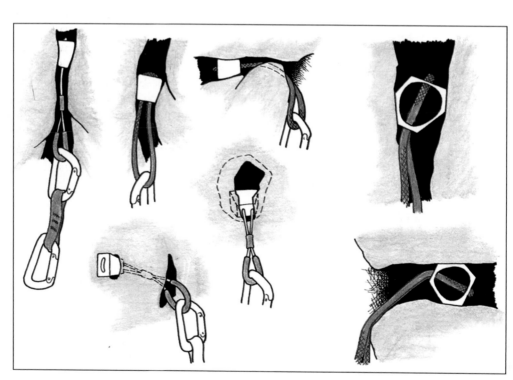

Various ways of placing a nut

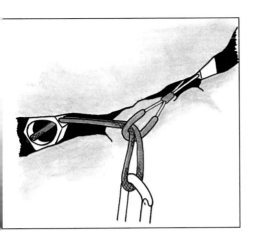

Nuts placed in opposition

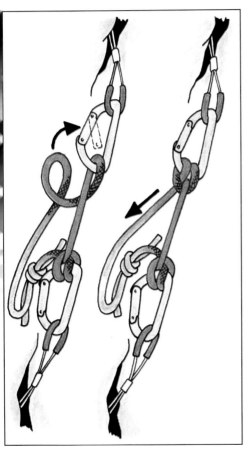

Placing two nuts in opposition by means of an adjustable clove hitch

direction they stay firmly in place. Check each nut by tugging it in the right direction;

▶ the nut must not be able to be lifted out of its placement by movement of the rope. Either select a crack that narrows in such a way that the nut cannot lift out, or wedge it in place by pulling on it as described above.

Nuts placed in opposition will stay in place if the pull is from several different directions. In order to place nuts in opposition, thread the sling of one nut through the wire loop or karabiner of the other. If the sling is not long enough, use another accessory cord or the rope. The correct tension is obtained by means of a clove hitch in the sling, which can be easily adjusted for tightness. This system is particularly useful at belay stations, where there may be several directions of pull.

If a nut is wedged in place so tightly that it cannot easily be removed, a nut removal tool (so-called "nutters" or "nut keys') will come in very handy. Use it either to lift the nut out or to dislodge it by tapping it.

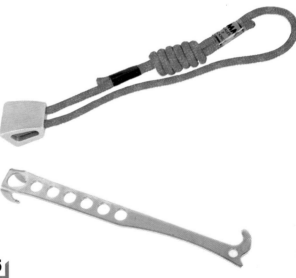

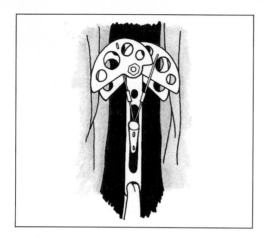

All four cams must be in contact with the rock

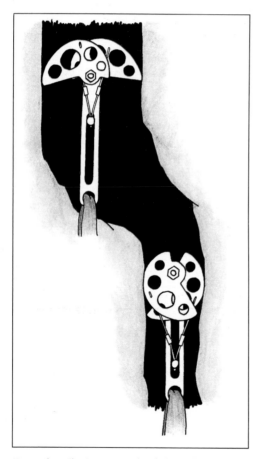

Excessive displacement (top), insufficient displacement (below)

Camming devices

Friends and other spring-loaded camming devices require a great deal of experience to place properly. What is more, it is not always easy to assess their reliability. It is worth bearing in mind the following points:

▶ all the cams must be in contact with the rock;

▶ displacement of the cams must lie within the optimal range. If the cam is too wide open (wide cracks), the wedging mechanism will no longer function and the device will be pulled out of place; if it is not opened out enough (narrow cracks), it will be virtually impossible to remove the expensive device;

▶ camming devices hold only in the direction of pull parallel to the cams. As a result, the stem must point in the anticipated direction of pull. Friends are generally unsuitable for use in situations in which there are several possible directions of pull (at belay stations, or in the event of a pendulum fall);

▶ the rock must be free of vegetation, soil or mud, otherwise the Friend will slide out of the crack;

▶ the crack must not open out at the back, since rope movements can make Friends

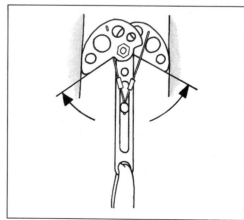

Optimal displacement

A Friend in place

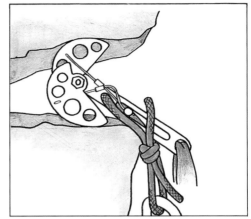

A rigid-stemmed Friend tied-off in a horizontal crack

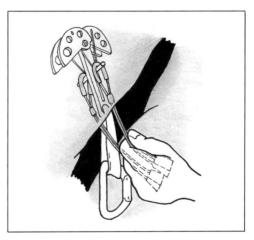

Removing a jammed Friend using the slings attached to two nuts

"walk" backwards into the crack. This may force the cams to open too wide;

▶ in horizontal placements, you should use devices with a flexible stem. If this is not possible, you must tie off the rigid stems.

If a Friend gets jammed into a narrow crack or "walks" back into the crack as a result of excessive rope movement, then removal can be problematic. In order to get at Friends that seem to be irretrievably lodged, you can place the slings of two nuts around the crosspieces and tug sharply, applying counter-pressure to the stem at the same time.

The same applies to sliders (devices with a pair of wedges in opposition) as to Friends. You should avoid placements in which the sliders are too close to each other and those in which the direction of pull is not parallel to the cable, as well as flared or muddy cracks.

Natural anchors

When looking for a point that can provide a solid anchor, nature has quite a lot to offer. As well as various rock formations and trees, many other features can also be used. However, assessment of their reliability as anchors requires a certain degree of circumspection and experience, and several points must be borne in mind before going ahead and using them. However, in general, most natural anchors are fairly reliable. The most frequently available anchors are outlined below, along with their uses and potential pitfalls.

Threads

Threads are usually bizarre features, where a hollowed out section of rock is bridged by a piece of dense rock, around which an accessory cord or sling can be placed. Its strength depends on its thickness and length. Short, thick bridges are obviously much more solid than long, thin ones.

As a rule of thumb, you can usually rely on bridges as thick as your arm, or thicker. You should examine the bridge and the surrounding rock for fine cracks: however thick it may be, only a thread without cracks makes a reliable anchor.

With very small or angled threads, it is best to use a stiff accessory cord made of Kevlar, Dyneema or Spectra. With larger threads, use loops of tubular tape. Threads can withstand force from any angle.

Various ways of using a thread as an anchor

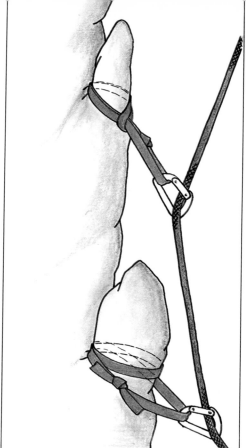

Using spikes as an anchor

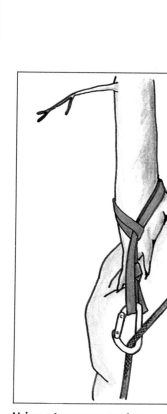

Using a tree as an anchor

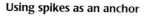

Spikes of rock

Spikes are small pillars of dense rock. They must be free of cracks and securely joined to the rock on which they stand. If there is any doubt at all, they should not, under any circumstances, be used as an anchor because in the event of a fall, the debris from the broken spike will pursue the falling climber and may hit him or her. If the spike consists of solid rock, attach a sling to it; the direction of pull can only be downwards, of course. In order to prevent the sling slipping off the spike, loop the sling round it twice and clip only one strand of rope into it. If the sling is long enough, you can also attach it with a lark's foot.

Trees

Trees 20 cm or more in diameter can normally be trusted, provided they have not been killed off by pollution. The ground in which they are rooted must also be borne in mind when assessing their suitability as anchors. Thinner trees and small shrubs may, at best, serve to boost morale; they should never be used as anchors.

In order to use a tree as an anchor, place a sling as low down as possible on the trunk and fix it in place with a lark's foot. This will prevent the sling from slipping and rubbing so that it eventually frays.

Cairns or crosses marking a summit and other suitable man-made structures can be used in the same way.

Anchoring

There will be times as a climber when you are at the rock face but not actually climbing. In this situation you are not protected from falling by your partner and so you must protect yourself, especially if you are in a position where there is a risk of falling. To do this, use the part of the rope leading away from the tie-in point and attach it to a locking karabiner with a clove hitch.

Double ropes can be used as a single rope by tying the two strands together into a karabiner. The karabiner can then be clipped on to an anchor, as described below (pp. 82–86), and locked (unless the locking mechanism is automatic).

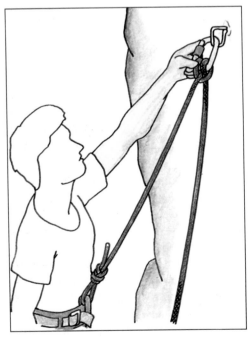

Anchoring the belayer

Belaying

Belaying carries with it a great deal of responsibility, since the life and well-being of your climbing partner depend on it. For this reason, you should always give it your utmost care and concentration.

The Munter or Italian hitch (HMS) is regarded as the safest method of belaying. This is a dynamic belay, which means that some rope is allowed to slip during severe falls. With a static belay, the entire energy of the fall, up to 1.2 tons, is absorbed very abruptly by the safety chain and the falling climber. With a dynamic HMS belay, the impact force is between 1 kN and 4 kN at most. However, it should be pointed out at this stage that the energy absorbed by the safety chain and the falling climber are dependent on many other factors including the quality of the rope management, the height of the fall, and so on.

Using a Munter hitch is very simple. Thread the rope through an HMS, which is an oversized pear-shaped karabiner with a locking gate (the mouth on other types of karabiner is not wide enough to keep the rope from binding when switching from taking in to feeding out rope) and attach it with a Munter hitch. If you are using a double rope, knot both strands together. The next section will explain where to attach the karabiner. In any event, you must make sure that the gate on the karabiner is locked. You can now pull the rope in both directions through the karabiner. When the direction of pull changes, the Munter hitch turns round automatically. The end of the rope leading to your climbing partner is the "live" end, while the other hand is called the "brake" end. By shuffling out the live end in short tugs and at the same time releasing the brake end, you can pay out as much rope as the climber needs. When belaying a top-roped

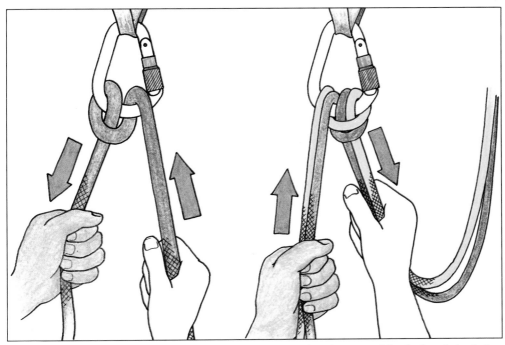

An Italian hitch belay with single and double ropes. Belaying the second (brake hand shaded, left), belaying the leader (brake hand shaded, right)

climber (p. 99), following the leader up the route and downclimbing, the rope is taken in in the opposite way. It is important never to let go of the brake end.

If the climber falls, the live end of the rope is immediately pulled downwards. The brake hand goes out and the hitch locks, stopping the rope running after a few centimetres or a metre at most, depending on the energy of the fall. This requires very little effort. However, if you do not act immediately, the rapidly moving rope may cause painful burns to your hand or, at worst, you may allow your partner to crash to the ground.

If the climber who has fallen is dangling from the rope, you can lower him or her to safety, or at least to the nearest "no hand rest" (i.e. a place where it is possible to stand up without hanging on), by carefully releasing the brake side of the rope and slowly paying it out. If this is not what the climber wants for one reason or another, perhaps because she wants to climb back up on the rope (p. 100), lock off the HMS by means of a slip knot.

Another method of belaying, used on practice crags, is to use a figure-of-eight descender. This method is very effective at absorbing the energy of a fall; the impact force is less than 2 kN, although the rope will run a considerably longer distance. The climber will also fall

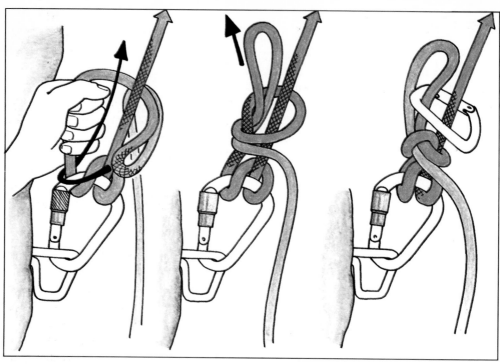

Locking a rope after a fall with the aid of a slipknot

further, and a lot of experience is required to hold a fall. A figure-of-eight device is wholly unsuited to belaying a second climber when the direction of pull is downwards, since the set-up does not provide enough friction. Moreover, the rapidity with which the rope runs through the belay device makes the use of a braking glove advisable in order to prevent rope burns or rope-handling errors. Thus a figure-of-eight descender should be used as a belay device only by experienced climbers to belay a leader climbing a practice crag. It is not a method for beginners.

In addition to these traditional methods, the industry has been working for some time on the development of automatic belay devices; however, they have yet to prove themselves.

Belaying the leader with a figure-of-eight descender

The belay station

The belay station is the foundation of the safety chain, since both climbers are ultimately protected by it. Thus it has two functions: to belay a companion and to secure the belaying climber. This is why a belay station must never fail. However, there is no generally applicable formula for setting up the optimal belay station, but rather a range of different methods to suit different situations.

Situation 1: Absolutely secure anchor
Firmly rooted, healthy trees more than 20 cm in diameter, expansion bolts that have been glued or cemented in place or those with external expansion sleeves are regarded as absolutely secure anchors. The same also applies to threads with bridges that are short, as thick as a human arm and free of cracks.
In order to set up a belay station, place a tape

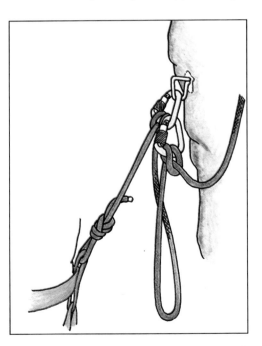

Belay station with protection for belayer and climber attached to a secure anchor

loop round a tree and secure it with a lark's foot. Clip the belayer's protection (locking karabiner with a clove hitch) into the loop and attach the HMS karabiner. The same method can be used with threads. The belayer's protection can also be clipped on to bolts, and the HMS karabiner can then be attached to the locking karabiner.

Situation 2: Two good anchors, up to 80 cm apart
Pitons in good condition and well placed, properly placed nuts (warning: the direction of pull at a belay station may be in several directions) and bolts with a minimum diameter of 10 mm (M10) are to be considered good anchors. Friends and other camming devices are less suitable for protecting a belay station, since the rope moves a great deal and there is a risk of the Friend sliding into an unfavourable position. For this reason, the two anchors are joined with a so-called triangle of forces. In order to distribute the load evenly between the two anchors, proceed as follows:
Clip the belayer's locking karabiner into one of the two anchors. Select the one likely to be the stronger. Now clip a standard karabiner on to both anchors. If the eye of the piton is too small to accept both the locking karabiner and the standard karabiner, clip the standard karabiner into the locking karabiner. Then attach a sling at least 120 cm in length and with a breaking strain of at least 20 kN to the two standard karabiners. The knot or stitching should be placed on one of the karabiners. Make a loop in one strand of the sling. Clip the HMS karabiner through the loop and over the strand of the sling. The loop in the sling is

important: if one of the anchors fails, the MS karabiner will not be able to slip out of the sling.

You must make sure that the angle at the apex of the inverted triangle does not exceed 90°, otherwise both anchors will be bearing more than 70 per cent of the total load. Indeed, if the angle is any greater than 90°, the load on the anchors will actually tend towards infinity.

Another method of equalizing the anchor is by using the central point method, in which you first construct the triangle of forces as described above. You then clip the belayer's locking karabiner into the triangle in the same way as described for the HMS karabiner. The HMS karabiner is then clipped into the belayer's karabiner.

The advantage of this method is that it exploits the potential of the belayer's body weight to absorb energy when the direction of pull is upwards. In this way, part of the impact force is absorbed as the belayer's body is lifted.

However, the disadvantages, indeed the danger of this method become apparent when the direction of pull is from the side. The belayer is then dragged sideways and will instinctively try to hold on to the rock

Belay station with load evenly distributed

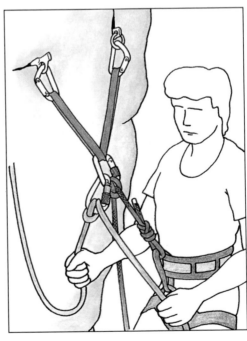

Central point method to equalize the anchor

or to brace herself against it. As she does so, she may well let go of the brake side of the rope.

Situation 3: Two or more good anchors, all of which are more than 80 cm apart

The triangle of forces arrangement cannot be used here, since the angle would be greater than 90°, unless you just happen to have an oversized sling to hand. Of course, you can always use the rope to extend the sling, but such arrangements usually make rope handling so problematic that they cannot be recommended.

The method usually adopted in such situations is the so-called "series connection". The locking karabiner is clipped into the strongest anchor with a clove hitch. The other anchors, each with a standard karabiner attached, are connected to the rope by means of a clove hitch. The HMS karabiner is clipped into the

belayer's locking karabiner, so that in the event of a fall the load is taken initially by the first anchor. If that fails, then the next one takes the strain, and so on.

Situation 4: The belayer is not at risk of falling at the bottom of a climb, where a good anchor is available. The distance between pitches is short, so possible fall distances are relatively short.

This is the commonest situation in sport climbing, since most routes are hardly any longer than the length of one rope. Thus the belayer stands on the ground at the bottom of the climb. Despite a great deal of disapproval, waist belaying has become the favoured method in such situations, largely because of the excellent rope handling.

The HMS karabiner is clipped straight into the tie-in loop on the belayer's sit harness, with her body substituting for a belay device. In order to prevent the belayer being lifted up in the event of a fall, thus increasing the fall distance for her partner, the belayer should be tied into an anchor, usually a tree. The line attaching the belayer can be considerably longer than her reach. The belayer should not stand directly at the bottom of the rock face, since in the event of a fall it would be impossible to avoid painful contact with the rock. However, if the belayer stands too far away from the face, she will be pulled horizontally towards the wall and be unable to use her body weight to arrest the fall. The angle between the base of the belayer's stance and the live end of the rope should, therefore, be no less than 60°. So if the belayer's anchor is located on the rock face or if the belayer is

A belay station with anchors in series

standing too far away from the face, one or other of the measures described above should be adopted.

Observation on practice crags would suggest that a lot of freeclimbers dispense with protection for the belayer. However, this is justifiable only if the belayer has sufficient experience in arresting falls, no falls longer than 5 m can occur and the difference in weight between the two climbing partners is no greater than 10 kg (if the belayer is heavier than the climber, this is of course no problem).

With or without protection for the belayer, waist belaying has a further significant advantage. As she arrests a fall, the belayer is lifted slightly upwards; this has the effect of reducing the impact force of the fall quite considerably. As a result, the rope, the falling climber and the entire safety chain are spared a great deal of shock loading.

Situation 5: Belaying the second, anchors set a long way back from the top of the route

This is also a common situation on practice crags. The problem with being tied to the belay anchor is that friction on the rope increases and contact with the second climber becomes difficult. In order to remedy this, lengthen the line attaching the belayer to the anchor. Clip the locking karabiner into the anchor. If the triangle of forces arrangement is being used, secure it as you would an HMS karabiner. Then extend the belayer's line (clove hitch in the locking karabiner) until you reach the edge of the cliff at the top of the route. Attach the HMS karabiner by means of a clove hitch to the section of rope between the belayer and the anchor so that it is within easy reach and use this arrangement to belay the second climber.

This method should be used only if the anticipated direction of pull is directly downwards, since there is a great risk of injury to both partners in the event of a pendulum fall. However, it can also be used in the middle of a route, not just at the top. To continue upwards, you will have to set up a new belay station directly adjacent to the anchors.

Waist belaying

60°

Belaying the second climber from an anchor set back from the top of the route

Runners

Runners are anchors placed during the climbing of a pitch (a section of climb between two belays and no longer than the length of one rope). They are necessary in order to reduce the length of any fall the leader might take. For example, if a freeclimber is scaling a wall at a height of 4 m above the ground, she would obviously hit the ground if she were to fall without any runners. If she places an anchor after 3 m, she will fall only twice the distance between herself and the anchor, i.e. 2 x 1 m = 2 m. However, this calculation does not include the stretching of the rope, the distance it travels in a dynamic belay before coming to a halt or any possible slack in the system. These factors will add a further 1 or 2 m to the fall. Thus our freeclimber would end up perilously close to the ground. It is therefore important that adequate pro-

Rope clipping into intermediate protection

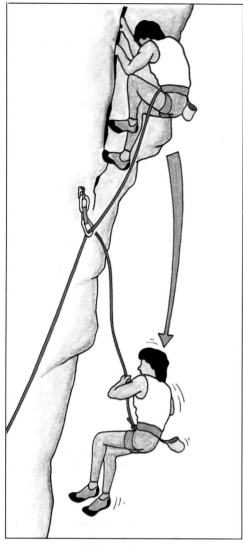

ferences in performance level between the two partners.

Depending on the difficulty of the climb and individual performance limits, runners can be placed every 1.5 to 5 m, as opportunities present themselves. You can use pre-existing anchors, such as pitons and natural rock features, or you can place nuts or Friends, etc. The load on an intermediate anchor may be up to 160 per cent of the impact force of a fall, since the energy of the live and brake ends of the rope is cumulative. The greatest care is also required when placing runners.

Clip a quickdraw with two karabiners or a sling into the anchor and then thread the rope through. The karabiner attached to the anchor should have a wide gate and be an asymmetrical D shape. A bent-gate karabiner can be used in the other loop on the quickdraw. The rope can be easily clipped in with one hand. The karabiners should be secured in the quickdraw with adhesive tape in order to prevent slipping and consequent sideways pulling.

You must make sure that the gate opening on the karabiner faces away from the rock, since

The length of a fall is twice the distance from the last piece of protection. Rope stretch, slack and braking distance all increase the length of a fall

tection should be placed at regular intervals. On traverses or diagonal stretches, runners are also important for the second climber, since without protection long pendulum falls are possible. A leader will have to take this into account when placing protection for her second, particularly when there are large dif-

A quickdraw

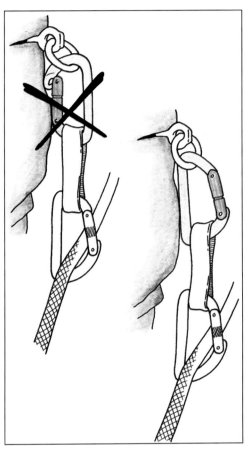

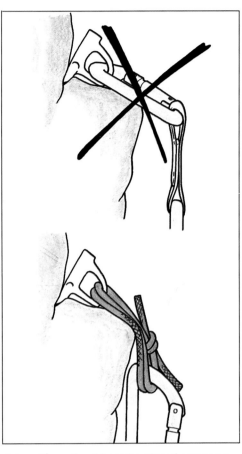

Incorrectly (left) and correctly placed protection

A karabiner should not be placed across an edge

in the event of a fall the gate might open, seriously reducing the karabiner's strength and possibly causing it to break. The karabiner is usually turned through 180° immediately after being clipped on to the anchor. Nor should the karabiner be placed across an edge, since it could buckle under strain. This can be avoided with the aid of a sling threaded through the anchor. Using just one or two karabiners without a quickdraw has the advantage of reducing the length of any possible fall, provided that rope handling is not impaired as a result.

The correct use of protection

Mastery of the individual protection techniques is a necessary but not sufficient condition for a safe climb. Only sensible application of the techniques and, above all, performing the necessary actions in the right sequence will ensure a trouble-free climb without excessive risk of a fall for either partner.

Let us now look more closely at a pair of climbers as they tackle a fairly lengthy route. Both of them are standing at the belay station.

Belaying

The belayer A has tied herself into an anchor. Her partner B is protected by the HMS and is beginning to climb. The belayer A must always be aware of the direction of pull on the rope in the event of a fall. If the leader B has not placed any intermediate protection, the direction of pull will be directly downwards. Once she has put protection in place (and the protection holds), the direction of pull will be directly downwards from the runner (i.e. at an oblique angle to the belayer). The belayer A must choose her stance accordingly, and the HMS must also be within reach when it comes under strain, otherwise it would be ripped out of her hand. She must also avoid becoming wedged between a taut rope and the rock, unable to act. This is particularly important when climbing traverses.

The belayer A pays out just the amount of rope required: the climber B should never feel the rope being tugged on from below, but conversely her fall distance must not be extended by unnecessary slack. In any event, the belayer must stay focused on the climber, who has the elements to contend with.

At the start of a pitch

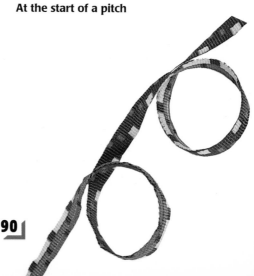

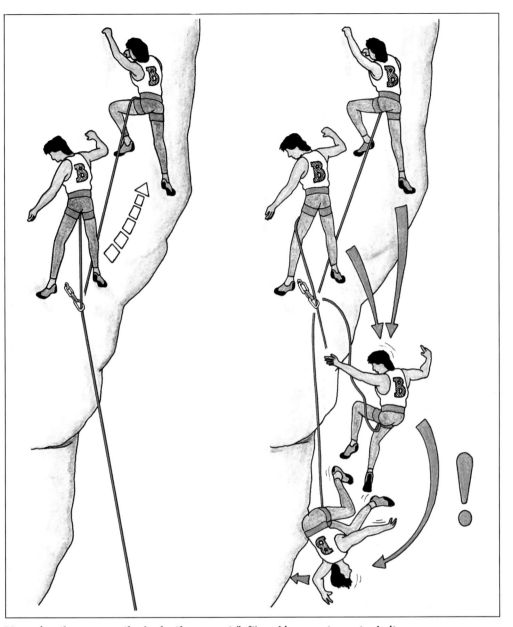

Managing the rope on the body: the correct (left) and incorrect way to do it

Handling the rope on the body

The leader B is now moving further and further away from the belay station; the rope leads down from her tie-in knot. In order to prevent one leg getting caught up in the rope and toppling the climber over backwards if she should fall, the rope leads downwards between her legs when she is climbing directly above the last runner and to one side of her body when she is climbing at an oblique angle to it.

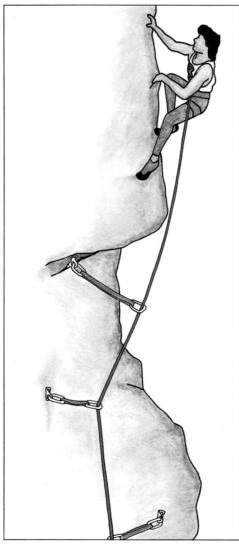

The rope should run up the cliff in a straight line

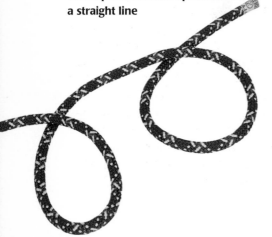

Handling the rope on the rock face

Depending on the difficulty of the climb, our leader B places runners at intervals of a few metres. In order to keep rope drag to a minimum, the rope must run in as straight a line as possible. If a piece of protection lies to one side of a rope leading down in a straight line, it can be extended by a sling of appropriate length.

Overhangs cause ropes to run crooked. In this case, long slings are clipped in just before the overhang and in the angle of the roof. If the rope gets too crooked, there may be nothing else for it but to climb back down to remove the offending piece of protection or to set up a belay station.

Protecting traverses

In order to prevent a pendulum fall above or below a traverse by the leader or her second, a piece of protection should be placed just before and just after the horizontal section. However, this often causes such an increase in rope drag that it is sensible to set up a belay station at the beginning or end of the traverse.

Changing belay station and climbing calls

Our leader has now done her best and is approaching the end of the pitch. The belayer A has already informed her by yelling "10 metres" and "5 metres" that only 10 and then 5 m of rope are left. If there is a risk of falling more than 10 m, the climber should not ascend right to the end of the rope in order to leave enough rope in reserve to arrest such a fall.

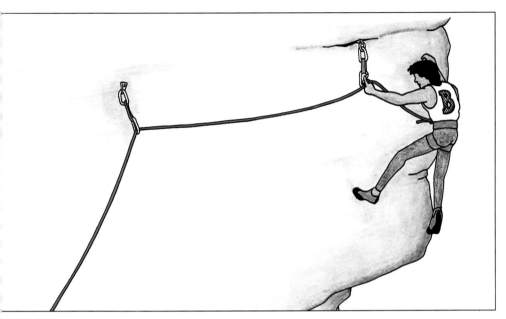

Protecting a traverse

The leader B has finally set up a belay station and tied herself in. She informs her partner A below by yelling "Safe". The belayer unclips the HMS and calls out "Take in". So B knows she is no longer protected by the HMS and can take in the rest of the slack, which she does without further ado. In order that leader B does not have to exert herself unnecessarily as she heaves on the rope, her companion A can shout out "That's me" when all the slack is taken in. The leader B now clips her partner into the HMS karabiner and calls out "Belay on". A now knows that she is being held by her partner and unclips herself from the anchor. She reminds the leader of her responsibilities by shouting out "Climbing" and begins her ascent.

Of course climbers do not necessarily have to use these calls, and they may agree on another system. However, in order to avoid misunderstandings, calls must be short, distinctive and agreed in advance. Even the uninitiated can recognize a pair of climbers

not used to each other's methods by their lengthy and noisy discussions about the imminent change of belay of station.

If a climber drops or dislodges anything down a cliff face, they must shout out very loud a warning to those below. The most popular calls are "BELOW", "ROCK", "WATCH OUT", and in Europe, "ATTENTION".

Belaying the second

The leader B pulls the rope through the HMS until all the slack is taken up but without climber A feeling any tugs. If there is still some slack in the system, A may ask her partner to take the rope in further by shouting out "Take in" or "Up rope". In hopeless situations, in which all hope of redpointing has to be abandoned on the spot, one may hear the failed climber gasp "Pull" as she requests assistance from her belayer. The call "Slack" or "Rope" means that more rope should be paid out.

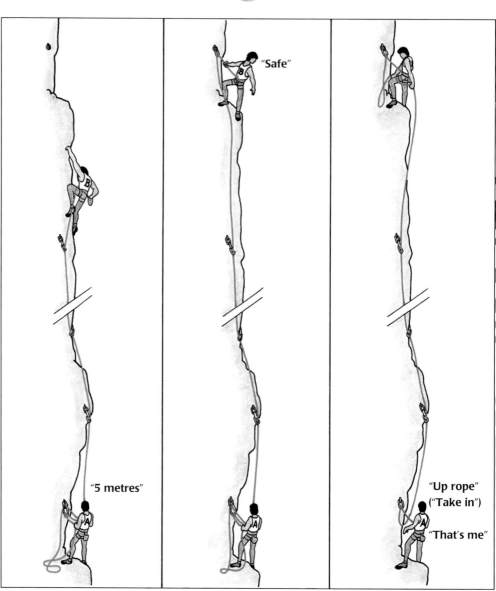

Changing belay station and climbing calls

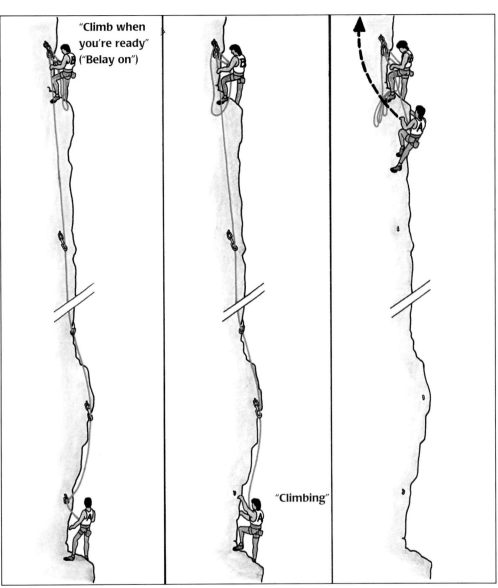

"Climb when you're ready" ("Belay on")

"Climbing"

The second climber A removes all the runners as she goes and eventually reaches the belay station. If she now takes over the lead, we talk of "swinging leads". The belayer B gives out some more rope, and the process begins all over again. However, if climber B is to lead on every pitch, the second ties herself into the anchor. The HMS is now transferred to climber B, who has until now been belaying. Then B unties herself from the anchor and begins to climb.

The most important principle in the whole enterprise is:

> Each climber must be secured at all times. A climber should not untie herself from an anchor until she is secured by her partner.

Tying in to the abseil anchor

Abseiling/rappelling

The usual way of getting down from the top of a steep climb is to abseil. This manoeuvre requires particularly assiduous attention, since tiredness or a lack of concentration often make themselves felt at the end of a climb. Several fatal accidents every year are proof of this.

Tying into the abseil anchor
Once you have set up the abseil anchor, tie yourself in with a ready-made sling about 60 cm to 1 m in length. Using a karabiner at either end, clip it on to the anchor and the tie-in loop on your sit harness.

Anchors
Only totally secure ("bombproof") anchors, such as bolts that have been cemented or glued in place or trees more than 20 cm in diameter, should be used for abseiling. Such anchors are usually already in place at frequently used abseil points. If this is not the case, you should not rely on any normal pitons you might find. Nor should you use slings left behind by other climbers. Placing an additional, secure anchor and renewing the slings will eliminate much of the risk involved in abseiling. Anything less could prove disastrous. If the bolt has a sufficiently large eye, simply thread the rope through. If there are several anchor points, connect them with a sling and then clip the rope into the sling.

If you are using a tree as an anchor, you can place a sling round the tree or attach the rope directly to it.

Setting the rope

If you are using a single rope, thread one end through the bolt or slings until the exact middle of the rope is anchored at the bolt or sling. Tie the two ends of the rope with an overhand knot so that you cannot slide off the end of the rope; this will also prevent one end of the rope slipping through the figure-of-eight belaying device and hurling the climber attached to the other end to the ground.

Now take the rope ends and throw them down the cliff, shouting out "Rope" as you do so, in order to warn any climbers or walkers who may be below. You must be tied into an anchor as you throw the rope, since you need to use both hands and the momentum of the throw may throw you off balance.

If the rope is not lying or hanging straight down the abseil route but is caught in a tangle a few metres below the abseil point, take it in and start the procedure all over again.

If you are using a double rope, tie the ends together with an overhand knot. The advantage of this knot is that it protrudes on one side only and can therefore usually be pulled over rough patches of rock rather than getting bound on them. When placing the knot on a ring or sling attached to the rock, you must make sure that the knot is on the strand of the rope running underneath the ring or sling. This will prevent the rope from jamming when pulled. The ropes can then be thrown down the cliff in the same way as a single one.

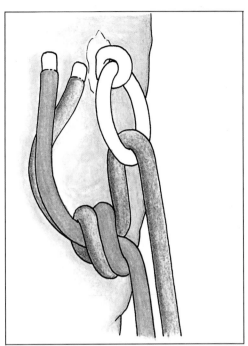

The correct way to thread the rope through the abseil anchor

Abseiling/rappelling

When you have set up the abseil point, thread a figure-of-eight descender on to the rope and attach it to the abseil anchor with a locking karabiner. Only at this point is it safe to untie yourself from the anchor. Position yourself directly under the anchor and reach out with one hand – the steadying hand – to the part of the rope leading to the anchor; place the other hand – the control or braking hand – on the rope below the descender. With your feet apart, lean back and put your weight on the rope and start to walk backwards down the cliff, pushing your body away from the rock with your feet as you do so. The weight of your body is borne by your

Abseiling with additional protection from a prusik knot

sit harness and the figure-of-eight descender. Your legs should be more or less at right angles to the cliff, which requires you to lean your whole body backwards, and will feel uncomfortable to begin with. The top hand is used merely for steadying purposes, while the lower hand is used to control the speed of descent. In order to avoid any unnecessary strain on the anchor, you should try to descend at an even pace and not to bounce or jump. The control hand must never let go of the rope. To halt your descent temporarily, move the control hand to one side or lock off the descender by tying a loop of slack rope into a simple hitch around the rope above the device.

Once you have reached the ground or ledge, first tie yourself into an anchor if you are still in a position from which a fall is possible. Then unclip the descender and inform your

partner above by shouting out "Rope free". It is advisable at this point to test the system by tugging on the rope in order to identify any possible problems with the anchor and to make sure that the rope is running smoothly down the cliff. The second climber then abseils down the cliff in the same way. Here too it is essential that each climber is secured at all times, either by being tied into an anchor or by having the descender threaded.

If the figure-of-eight descender has been lost or forgotten, you can use an HMS karabiner for abseiling. At the abseil point, attach the karabiner to the double rope with a clove hitch. From this point onwards, the procedure is the same as with a figure-of-eight descender. However, since this method increases the rope's tendency to kink, thus placing a great deal of strain on it, it should be used in emergencies only.

Protecting yourself while abseiling

If the climber is overtired or inexperienced in the abseil technique, or if conditions are otherwise unfavourable, it is advisable to use some form of additional protection. A prusik loop can be fixed around both abseil ropes below the descender with a 4 or 5 mm accessory cord. It can then be clipped into the tie-in loop on your harness by means of a karabiner. However, the loop should not be long enough to get pulled into the descender. The control hand is placed around the prusik loop as you descend. If you let go, the rope will lock.

Pulling the rope down

Once both partners have reached a safe position, untie the safety knot at the end of the rope and pull on one end to retrieve it. If you are using a double rope, you should have noted the colour of the rope on which you have to pull in order to prevent the knot getting caught in the anchor.

Top-roping

A top rope is essentially a belay from above. Such an arrangement is particularly suitable for novices and freeclimbers performing close to the limits of their technique, and has become firmly established as a belay method in attempts to improve performance in sport climbing circles.

The technique can be very similar to that used to protect a second (p. 93), in other words, the climber is protected from above from a belay station at the top of the climb. However, since very many routes on practice crags are shorter than half a rope's length, the rope can be run through an anchor placed at the top of the climb (a bolt fixed in with glue or cement, or a tree with a sling placed round it) and back down to the ground. The rope is clipped into the anchor, just as for abseiling. However, there is one significant difference: the rope must never be attached directly to a sling. Rather, it must be threaded through a karabiner, since the friction generated would simply cut through a sling and the climber would be hurled to the ground.

The climber attaches herself to one end of the rope and the belayer clips the HMS into the tie-in loop on her harness. No further protection is needed for the climber, since a fall can be no longer than the stretch in the rope.

Once the climber has successfully reached the top of the crag, or been defeated by fatigue or lack of technique, the belayer can lower her by slowly and smoothly releasing the brake side of the rope. A climber being lowered in this way should adopt the same

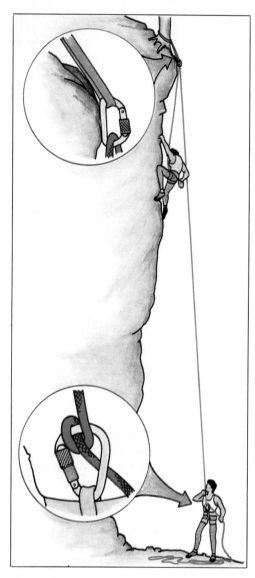

Top-roping. The rope must never run directly through the sling, but must be threaded through a karabiner

posture as for abseiling. If the descent is jerky, the fault may lie with the belayer's rope-handling or with her partner's posture. If the latter holds on to the cliff from time to time or descends with her feet pointing down, the rope is not kept constantly taut, making the descent uncomfortably jerky.

As already mentioned, letting a climber down from a top-rope belay places severe strain on the rope.

Climbing up a fixed rope

In an emergency, it is also possible to climb up a 9 or 11 mm rope. Such a situation might arise if you are following up an overhang, come off a hold, swing away from the rock and are left dangling in space. You have two options: to be lowered to the ground if it is near enough, or to climb up the rope. You should first practise climbing up a rope in a controlled situation. Perhaps the best way of doing this is to abseil down a cliff and then climb back up again while the rope is still securely in place. There are two methods of ascending a rope:

1. Prusik loops: take some 4 mm cord and make two slings tied with a double fisherman's knot, one about 20 cm and the other 60 cm in length. Tie both slings on to the rope at around waist height with a prusik knot, placing the shorter one above the longer. Then use a locking karabiner to attach the shorter one to the main loop in your harness.

Place one foot – whichever feels more comfortable – in the longer loop and press down. The rope will then stretch considerably. When it rests on the floor, slide the knot of your waist prusik up the rope, as far

An ascender fitted between sit and chest harness as a means of climbing up a fixed rope

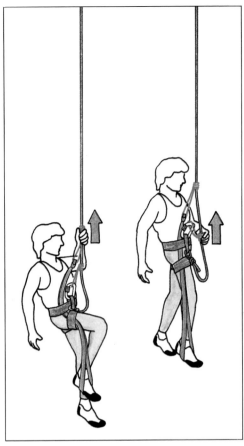

Climbing up a dangling rope with the aid of two prusik loops

as it will go. Now sit back in your harness to take up the stretch.

Release the foot prusik and slide it up to the waist prusik knot; removing your foot from the loop may make this easier. Now repeat the procedure. Standing up in the footloop, reach up with one hand and grasp the rope; with the other, release the waist prusik knot and slide it up the rope.

This is the standard prusik method, and every effort should be made to master it. There are various other methods involving the use of smaller slings, such as the cord from any nut runners you may have. It is also possible to run a sling through the harness in order to aid balance.

2. Ascenders: potholers and those who work on high buildings do a lot of rope climbing, but they prefer to use an ascender clipped into a waist and shoulder harness. Such a device supports you in the standing position, and slides up the rope without assistance when you stand up. It makes ascending very easy and is worth experimenting with.

Training

If the following pages create the impression that a climber's training consists solely of tedious exercises, the impression is neither correct nor intended. Our aim, rather, is to outline a supplementary training programme for climbers with sporting ambitions that will complement the mileage they actually do on the rocks.

However, before launching into the first training section, a few things should be clarified. For example, what is training exactly?

Sports scientists define the term as follows:

Training is a systematic process, carried out on the basis of scientific findings, the objective of which is the all-round development of physical, coordinative, psychological and intellectual capacities, as well as technical skills, as a means of establishing the conditions for sporting performance.

Not all definitions are illuminating – and this one is no exception. So, to clarify matters further:

Fitness is the sum total of all the factors that determine sporting performance; the term is also used to denote psychological and physical condition. It can be divided up into the various individual physical capacities: endurance (the capacity to resist fatigue), strength (the capacity to overcome resistance through muscular contraction) and speed (the capacity to make rapid movements or to advance quickly).

These three basic physical qualities also exist in hybrid forms (power-endurance, speed-endurance, power), which suggests they are mutually dependent.

Flexibility (which denotes the range of possible movement around a joint) and dexterity (which refers to manipulative skills and physical coordination) are also part of the definition of fitness. Being in good condition means having the ability to react and adapt, a good sense of control, direction and balance, good reasoning power, nimbleness and agility.

Coordinative capacities are more or less synonymous with dexterity and require no further explanation here.

Psychological capacities or qualities include phenomena such as strategic memory, alertness and attentiveness, together with speed and precision of sensor-motor reactions, all of which combine to produce intellectual capability.

This group of qualities, signified by the general term "mental sphere", has become a focus of attention in recent years, and is always trotted out as an explanation when no physical cause can be found for a particular event or phenomenon. Nevertheless, there is no doubting the close, perhaps decisive relationship between physical and mental fitness.

Technical skills, finally, are the sequences of moves or actions developed on the basis of a sportsperson's physical and psychological abilities that have to be performed in the course of a particular sporting activity. Over time, and with continuous practice, they become a virtually automatic part of the motor processes.

Tactics or tactical behaviour are also part of the training process. However, we shall go into this in greater detail later. To summarize:

> Training is a systematic process designed to improve fitness, technical skills and tactical awareness as well as mental and psychological capabilities.

So we have laid the theoretical foundations of training. But what aspects of all this should a sport climber concentrate on when trying to improve his or her performance? What demands does the sport of freeclimbing make on an athlete's physical and mental make-up and what is the structure of the sport's demand profile?

The demand profile

The aim of freeclimbing is to climb routes in the highest possible grade of difficulty on rock or on artificial climbing walls. The difficulty of any particular climb, irrespective of gradient, the size of foot and handholds or the distance between them, is assessed by the first climber and then commented upon and adjusted by subsequent climbers. Thus a climber's performance depends to a large extent on the development of his or her technical skills. Mastery of climbing techniques and the concomitant ability to control the body's centre of gravity – which is dependent to a large extent on coordinative abilities – form the basis of a climber's performance.

However, technique alone will get nobody up a rock face; basic physical qualities have to be brought into play, above all three different aspects of strength. The first of these is power-endurance, which is the ability to expend strength over a long period without tiring; the second is maximum strength, needed to surmount particularly difficult features on a climb; the third is power, required for dynamic climbing.

Flexibility also plays an important role, since it extends the range of techniques available to a climber and makes it possible to use the limbs for climbing even in unusual positions.

Finally, general endurance – the efficiency of the cardiovascular system – is important for

climbers when climbing in high alpine locations, both because of the altitude and the length of the approach routes and climbs. Moreover, general endurance is the basis of all training, since it creates and sustains general physical fitness, increases training overload and therefore contributes to healthy training.

However, the rapid development of mountaineering into the modern, competitive sport of climbing has meant that the notion of all-round physical training has often been grossly ignored. As a result, some younger climbers, in seeking to push their performance to extremes, have adopted such one-sided training regimes that they have developed severe muscular imbalances that have given rise to postural anomalies, quite apart from the stress injuries they suffer, particularly to the finger joints. The most difficult routes used to be on sheer walls; they are now to be found on overhangs, and this shift prompted sport climbers to build up only those muscle groups needed for such climbs. As a result, many of them developed the round-shouldered posture that has become almost a trade mark. However, the correct approach, in this case as in most others, is to work not only on the muscles most used on difficult overhangs but also on their antagonists (example: biceps = arm flexor muscle; triceps = arm extensor muscle). All-round physical training also requires the rigorous pursuit of improved flexibility through stretching exercises involving all muscle groups and joints; unfortunately, such exercises are regarded all too often as an ordeal to be avoided if at all possible.

In addition to the physical factors that determine performance, the demand profile of freeclimbing also includes psychological factors such as overcoming any fear of heights or of falling, the ability to withstand pain, for example on very small handholds, and to develop will power in training, as well as skills in route planning as well as tactical behaviour.

Having made clear what a climber must be able to do, we now need to discover how he can achieve what is required. The individual sections in this chapter are arranged in the same sequence as they would occur in a training session: warm-up, flexibility, climbing technique, power, maximum strength, power-endurance and general endurance. There is also a short section on mental training and some hints on nutrition. However, this most certainly does not mean that each of these components must be included in every training session. It makes much more sense, in fact, to focus on just one or two components per session.

Warming up

Any sporting activity, whether training or competition, should always be preceded by a warm-up. A distinction is usually made between general and specialized warm-ups, but the purpose of both is to prepare the body for work.

The function of a general warm-up is to activate the cardiovascular and metabolic systems and to stimulate hormone production. It is intended to warm the body up for performance, while a specialist warm-up, which always follows a general warm-up, helps to activate the muscle groups most frequently used in climbing and to fine-tune energy supplies and the nervous system. Such a warm-up programme should never last less than 20 minutes, and should usually take about half an hour.

General warm-up

Always begin your general warm-up with light jogging or skipping until you begin to feel warm or start to sweat slightly. This should be followed by stretching exercises, as outlined in the section on flexibility training (p. 107), that bring into play all the important joints and muscle groups (calves, thighs, hips, trunk, shoulders, arms, fingers, neck). You should focus next on strengthening individual muscle groups, particularly those in the trunk, which are frequently neglected. Three examples are given below.

Strengthening the stomach muscles
Lying on your back, bend your hips and knees until they are at right angles to your body. Then, with your arms crossed on your chest, curl your shoulders and chest towards your knees and then relax them down to the floor again.

Strengthening the lower back muscles
Lying on your back, bend your knees and bring your feet towards your body. Now raise your hips from the floor and point your toes up away from the floor. Then stretch first the left, then the right leg parallel to the thigh of the supporting leg.

Strengthening the upper back muscles
Lying on your back, bend your arms and place them on the ground close to your body. Contract the muscles in your upper back and lift your body off the ground, using your elbows for support.

After these fairly gentle warm-up exercises, you could increase your heart rate by doing a few knee-bends and stretches and some skipping, before moving on to the specialized warm-up exercises.

Strengthening the stomach muscles

Specialized warm-up

The best way of warming up specifically for climbing is bouldering. Make sure you start on easier sequences and work up gradually to tougher ones, so that your fingers have time to adjust to the increasing strain. Most of the injuries sustained in sport climbing could be avoided if this simple rule were obeyed. Climbing familiar routes is also a good way of warming up, but go up little by little. If you climb up high, particularly after a long lay-off, fears and inhibitions can lead to muscle tension. For safety and comfort you should try to avoid this happening, and a good warm up should help to loosen and relax you.

Strengthening the lower back muscles

Strengthening the upper back muscles

Flexibility training

Inadequate flexibility restricts the range of techniques available to a climber and increases the risk of injury. So one of the crucial aims of training is to improve flexibility in all the joints.

The degree of flexibility is determined by the limit of a joint's range of movement, the pliability of tendons and ligaments and the elasticity of the muscles responsible for moving the joint; the first factor is anatomically fixed, the second cannot be influenced by training, but the third can be affected to a considerable degree by the right exercises.

The stretching method is a tried and tested way of improving flexibility. It is based on the fact that a muscle that is stretched too much is forced to contract by its protective reflex, thus preventing it from being stretched. In order to bypass this reflex mechanism, the muscle to be stretched is contracted isometrically (for between 8 and 10 seconds), then relaxed (for about 1 second) and finally placed in the position that causes stretching pain and held there (for about 20 seconds).

In order to achieve any improvement at all in flexibility, you must have a flexibility training session at least three times per week. However, only with daily practice will you achieve optimal results.

It is of course possible to make mistakes in flexibility training: jerky or sweeping expansive movements, for example the popular leg swings, can lead to very minor injuries – so-called micro-traumas – that may develop later

Training for optimal flexibility helps to extend the range of techniques and motion available to a climber

Stretching the calf muscles

Stretching the knee flexor muscles

Stretching the thigh extensor muscle

into more serious injuries, or even permanent damage. This is why all exercises should be performed slowly and, as far as possible, passively, and why the insertion and origin of the muscle should be not be moved too far apart once the point is reached at which stretching pain sets in. However, a slight twinge in the muscle is not an indication of over-extension; on the contrary, it is essential if any improvement in flexibility is to be achieved. But if you feel an unpleasant pain at the insertion, then the muscle has already been stretched beyond its maximum limit and there is a risk of injury.

Some flexibility exercises for climbers
Stretching the calf muscles
In the press-up position, and with the legs bent at the hips, place one foot on the back of the calf of the other leg, with the instep lying flat. Stretch the supporting leg, pressing the heel into the floor.

Stretching the adductors

Stretching the adductors and the lower back

Stretching the lateral muscles

Stretching the knee flexor muscles
Stand with one foot a long step in front of the other and fully stretched. Slowly lower your shoulders towards your outstretched leg. Stop moving at the point at which you feel your back is fully extended.

Stretching the thigh extensor muscle
Stand with your feet together and your legs straight. Lift one foot up towards your buttock and hold it there with both hands. Now place both knees parallel to each other and push the hips forward to extend the stretch.

Stretching the adductors
Sit on the floor with your back straight and your legs stretched out in front of you, then place the soles of your feet together and draw your feet towards your body as far as possible. Now press your thighs against the floor to complete the stretch.

Stretching the adductors and the lower back muscles
Sit on the floor with your legs bent. Gradually press the right thigh towards the floor pulling the foot as close as possible to your body. Now cross the left leg over the right, placing the left foot close to the knee. Now twist your trunk towards the left and support yourself against its outside edge with your upper arm in order to hold the stretch.

Stretching the lateral muscles that extend the spine
Standing with your legs apart, lean your body over to one side, keeping your hip straight and centred. Now stretch your upper right arm horizontally along the axis of your body.

Stretching the pectoral muscles
Stand with your feet hip-width apart, stretch the right arm out at shoulder height and place your hand, palm upwards, against a wall. Twist your body until you are away from the wall and looking over your left shoulder.

Stretching the finger flexor muscles
Place your hands palms together in front of you, with the tips of your fingers pointing upwards. Now move your hands down until the palms of your hands are forced slightly apart.

Stretching the finger extensor muscles
Stretch your arms out horizontally on either side of your body with your palms facing downwards. Without moving your wrists, clench your fingers to form a fist.

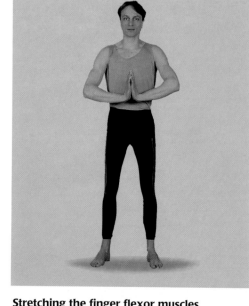

Stretching the finger flexor muscles

Stretching the pectoral muscles

Stretching the finger extensor muscles

Practising your technique

The purpose of training to improve your technique is to consolidate and extend your repertoire of movements. In this way techniques that have already been fully or partially mastered are practised, while new techniques are acquired. New techniques can be achieved in two ways:

Holistic-analytic: each move is practised in its entirety; mistakes are analysed and individual components of the move practised separately in order to perfect the entire move.

Reductionistic-synthetic: the technique is broken down into its various components, which are then practised separately before the entire sequence is rehearsed from start to finish. This is the method adopted here.

A great deal of patience is needed to acquire a new climbing technique, particularly when it involves frequent repetition of the same movement, firstly to eliminate serious errors and then to fine-tune the technique. An artificial climbing wall is particularly suitable for practising new techniques, not least because natural rock should not be reduced to a piece of gymnastic equipment. The ideal climbing site for training purposes is one that can be varied slightly to take account of differences in body size and build.

The rest of this section will focus on one technique in order to illustrate the method used to learn it.

Stepping on to a high-lying foothold

Technique: Stepping on to a high-lying foothold on a vertical wall.

The move can be broken down into the following components: lifting the leg; stepping on to the hold and exerting downward pressure on it and transferring weight to the new foot placement; and finally straightening up the body.

Phase 1: Lifting the leg can be practised on wall bars, for example, by trying to place one foot on the highest bar without any assistance from the arms. Practise with the right and left legs alternately and gradually increase the height of the bar you are aiming for. Finally, measure the height of the highest bar you have managed to reach.

Phase 2: Fasten a large foothold on to a vertical or sharply-angled wall, about 30 cm

111

below the height you have just measured. Your aim is to place one foot on the hold and maintain balance without any support from your hands. If you manage the move at this height, raise the foothold to the height you achieved on the bars.

Phase 3: When straightening up the body, it is permissible to begin by pulling yourself up by the arms before mastering the ideal form of the move, which is to bring yourself into the standing position simply by pushing up with your legs, without any assistance from a handhold. When you can perform the three phases of the move equally well with both the left and the right feet, you should try the complete sequence in order to practise coordinating the individual components. Once the whole technique has been mastered, you can strengthen and consolidate your newly acquired skill by repeated practice.

Training for power

Averaged over the year, power training occupies only relatively little space in a climber's training schedule. It is interesting to note that excessive maximum strength training actually reduces a climber's power, which has to be built up again after a hard winter's training. So this form of training does not form part of the training schedule until the spring, when a climber wants to get into shape for dynamic rock climbing.

Any training intended to improve a climber's power should be preceded by a maximum strength test, which measures the maximum force an athlete exerts in an exercise that he can perform just once by expending all his strength. The result of the maximum strength test provides the basis for determining the training load.

Power denotes the ability of an athlete to overcome resistance by contracting the muscles at high speed. As already noted, it is used mainly in dynamic climbing. Maximum strength is the determinant of power (p. 113), but in the training process, high maximum strength is associated with reduced speed of movement because of the extremely high additional loads it places on the body. This is why it is recommended that these two aspects of strength should be developed alternately. In neither case should training give rise to excessive fatigue, since that would prevent the central nervous system being stimulated.

The following method can be used to improve power once a high maximum strength has been achieved:
Sets of explosive exercises requiring 30 to 50 per cent of maximum strength should be repeated six to ten times. The pause between each set should be two to five minutes, while the number of sets per training session and exercise should be between four and six.

It is even possible to simulate something close to power training during an actual climbing session. A climber can use techniques he has already mastered well and that are suitable for making rapid moves on the rock face. The main phase of the move should therefore be as explosive as possible. During this phase, the muscles involved are subjected to extremely high loads. So you should always warm up properly with stretching exercises and should never embark on power training when tired. This means that such training should never be preceded either by maximum strength or endurance training.

Training for maximum strength

Maximum strength is the maximum force a muscle can exert at any one time. The form of training best suited to improving maximum strength involves high to maximum muscle tension combined with relatively long durations for each individual contraction. A distinction is made between, on the one hand, absolute and relative strength (i.e. strength as a function of body weight) and, on the other, three different kinds of work done by the muscles, all of which occur regularly in freeclimbing:

▶ "concentric" contraction, which occurs when the muscle shortens while producing a force (e.g. when pulling the body up);

▶ "eccentric" contraction, which occurs when the muscle lengthens while still producing a force (e.g. when letting the body down);

▶ "isometric" contraction, which occurs when the body does not move and the muscle involved remains the same length (e.g. the work done when locked off on a hold).

Training for dynamic power

"Concentric" and "eccentric" contractions are also known as "dynamic work". The best way of exercising the muscles for dynamic work is through so-called pyramid training. Once the maximum strength has been established, the following exercise schedule should be completed:

8 to 10 repetitions at 80% of max. strength
4 to 6 repetitions at 90% of max. strength
2 to 3 repetitions at 95% of max. strength
1 repetition at 100% of max. strength
2 to 3 repetitions at 95% of max. strength
4 to 6 repetitions at 90% of max. strength
8 to 10 repetitions at 80% of max. strength

Thus the pyramid is built up on one side, to be descended on the other. The pauses between the sets of repetitions should be not less than two minutes. When changing over to another exercise or to another piece of equipment, the break should be between three and five minutes. It is important when training for maximum strength, and particularly so for climbers, not to spend too much time on exercises requiring less than 80 per cent of maximum strength, since this leads to an increase in muscle mass and therefore body weight; with exercises requiring more than 80 per cent of maximum strength, on the other hand, the increased strength manifests itself rather in improved neuromuscular coordination, which is beneficial to the development of the relative strength that is so important to climbers.

A practical tip: strength training, particularly in the submaximal and maximal regions and when using free weights, should not be done without a partner to support and, if necessary, assist you.

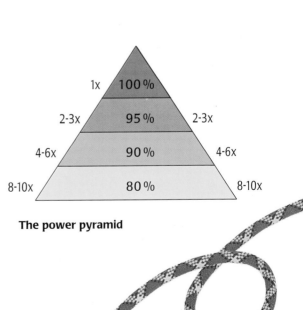

The power pyramid

Isometric power training

Isometric capacity is important to the climber in all situations in which he is not moving upwards but gripping a handhold, holding the body in a particular position in order to survey the rock ahead of him for holds, etc.

Isometric exercise involves an increase in muscle tension without any lengthening or shortening of the muscle. This is best done by applying pressure against stable resistance, with the joints bent at various angles, with 80 to 100 per cent of maximum contractility being used and each contraction lasting between five and ten seconds.

Once again, it is worth stressing that all-round physical training requires that isometric exercises should not be confined to those muscles important in climbing moves (agonists), but should also include their antagonists if postural problems are to be avoided.

Muscle strengthening exercises for climbers

The maximum force a muscle can exert can be increased only by making it bear additional weight. That additional weight can be provided either by metal discs attached to long or short dumb-bells or by so-called "multigyms", as found in fitness centres, gyms or many a private exercise room. Sometimes there is also a simple solution that can be adopted.

In all the following exercises, it is the "concentric" contraction of the particular muscle that is described. The "concentric" contraction required to return the muscle to its original position before repeating the exercise takes place in the reverse order to that described.

For a concentric contraction, breathe out, and for an eccentric contraction, breathe in.

Strengthening the leg extensor muscles

In the sitting position and with the back held straight, hook your feet round the handles. The axis of rotation of the knees and of the machine should be at the same height. Now stretch your legs, keeping your back straight as you do so.

Strengthening the leg flexor muscles

Lying on your stomach, hook your legs around the handles. Now bend your legs as far as possible. The leg flexors act as antagonists to the extensors.

Strengthening the pectoral muscles and the latissimus

Grab the handle with both hands and pull it down to your thighs. Important: keep your back flat on the bench!

Strengthening the latissimus

Grasp the levers with both arms outstretched. Now push the arms down through a semicircle, keeping the elbows straight.

Strengthening the pectoral muscles and the arm extensors

Lie on your back on the bench, with your legs bent. Take the weights out of the holder and briefly raise them straight up in the air with your arms outstretched. Now lower your arms to your chest and then raise them again.

Strengthening the pectoral muscles

Place your arms against the cushioned levers. Keeping your back straight, push your arms together until the levers almost meet.

Strengthening the upper back muscles

Lie face down on an inclined bench. Grip the weights and lift them until your arms form an angle of 90°. The upper back muscles are the antagonists of the pectoral muscles.

Strengthening the leg extensor muscles

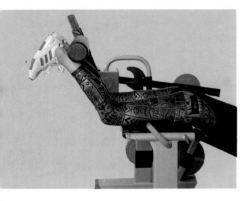

Strengthening the leg flexor muscles

Strengthening the pectoral muscles and the latissimus

Strengthening the latissimus

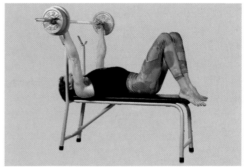

Strengthening the pectoral muscles and the arm extensors

Strengthening the pectoral muscles

Strengthening the arm flexor muscles

Rest your upper arms against the pads of the machine. Grip the lever with your arms out-stretched and your palms facing inwards. Bring your arms as close as possible to your face.

Strengthening the arm extensor muscles

Again, rest your upper arms against the pads of the machine. Grip the lever with your arms outstretched and your palms facing down-wards. Now push your arms down as far as you can. In technical terms, with this exercise the extensor on the back of the upper arm is the antagonist of the flexor.

Strengthening the finger flexors

Get a firm rubber ring or ball, or a tennis ball and squeeze it repeatedly to strengthen your fingers and hands.

Strengthening the arm flexor muscles

Strengthening the arm extensor muscles

Strengthening the upper back muscles

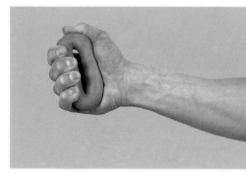

Strengthening the finger flexors

Strength-Endurance training

Strength-endurance is the capacity to withstand fatigue while expending strength over a long period of time. The essential condition for effective strength-endurance training is that as much work as possible should be done against greater resistance than is normally encountered in the conditions specific to the sport. It consists largely of special exercises based on the moves specific to the sport in question but designed to make the basic conditions (in this case, a low to medium level of overload) more difficult. A distinction is made between general and local endurance. The latter is more important for climbers, since one of the fundamental aims of training for freeclimbing is to increase the local endurance of the finger flexor muscles (this muscle group is located wholly in the forearm), without which climbing in the upper performance range would be impossible.

The method outlined below is a tried and

The strength and endurance of the finger flexor muscles are crucial to a climber's performance

tested way of improving a climber's power-endurance; it is illustrated by taking the example of the pull-up.

Beginners should hang from a bar using a standard grip and with the hands extended a good way beyond the shoulders. The exercise begins with a number of pull-ups (80 per cent of the highest number previously achieved). On the last pull-up, the climber holds his position at the top of the pull for about eight seconds. He then lowers his body but without fully extending his arms and holds that position for a further eight seconds (training in will-power!).

He follows this with another pull-up, after which he lets himself down slowly. After a break of about two minutes, the exercise is repeated.

Advanced climbers should already be beginning to pay special attention to training their finger flexors. Finger or hang boards have proved themselves as the best piece of equipment for this purpose. Having evolved from wooden bars into moulded plastic devices designed for practising various forms of pull-up, they have now developed further into large and very versatile pieces of equipment. A hang board suitable for improving the strength of the finger flexors should provide holds of various shapes and degrees of steepness. The

Hang boards have proved to be the best way of strengthening the finger flexor muscles

latest development, a training device for home use that incorporates an overhanging climbing area, is already commercially available. Training on hang boards should also be conducted in accordance with the principle outlined above.

If the training device makes it possible to simulate small sequences of holds, then a few combinations of moves could be performed, followed by some more pull-ups with the climber again holding his position at the top of the last pull and finishing of the exercise with an eccentric contraction. This may be either a simple let-down from the pull-up or a more complex sequence of movements (on the piece of equipment shown below left, for example, the climber could let himself down slowly from the head of the snake via the individual coils of its body).

Athletes training for competition do strength-endurance training based on the same principle, although with additional workloads. The additional load should be high enough for about twelve repetitions to be sufficient for fatigue to set in, while holding a position for about six to eight seconds should cause complete exhaustion. Despite this, the let-down should be as slow as possible.

General endurance training

A high level of general endurance is the basis of all training and should be part of any training programme throughout the whole year. The recommended methods are, in summer, cross-country running and cycling and, in winter, cross-country skiing. Each period of exercise should last not less than 40 minutes.

Mental training

The mental problems associated with free-climbing are enormous, and even climbers with experience at the very highest level will admit that they have had to overcome psychological difficulties on serious routes, even if they have climbed them before. It can be assumed from this that it is certainly no easier for beginners and that a certain degree of stress is always associated with each new problem that has to be overcome.

The basis of any athlete's self-confidence is certainly belief in his own ability. Thus the ideal mental state for climbing would be total concentration. However, since there is always a fear of falling, particularly when a climber is seeking to push his technique to the limits, concentration is always somewhat impaired. However, since the human psyche can be influenced by training, improvement is possible. Learning how to deal with fear and how to relax voluntarily in order to be able to concentrate on the activity in hand – namely climbing – are the basic aims of any such training. The methods employed are various forms of psychological self-regulation, which can only be listed here. They include autogenic and psycho-muscular training, desensitization, restoration of strength and energy, activation and mental training. Other methods of improving concentration and relaxation include meditation and yoga. All these methods have one thing in common: it takes time to learn them, let alone apply them, and they usually require the guidance of a teacher.

Skill brings with it increased confidence

Seasonal scheduling

Training is a systematic process designed to improve an athlete's all-round and specific performance. Starting from the recognition that not all the components of sporting performance can be developed at once and that a period of recovery is essential after an athlete has reached peak performance level, a general, somewhat loosely structured annual training schedule can be constructed as follows: preparation period, competition period, transitional period. This general structure can also be repeated once or twice in the course of the year and altered to suit individual requirements. In the preparation period, the general foundations are laid, with relatively high volume and low workloads. In the competition period, the main objective is the development of specific capacities, with considerably higher workloads and lower volume. The purpose of the transitional period is regeneration through active recovery, so there is absolutely no point in training all-year round without a break and without changing the nature of the training. Greater improvements in performance can be achieved through carefully planned and targeted periods of training and recovery. In general, it is advisable to have a break from training in the late autumn. As the days get shorter and the rock no longer retains much warmth and when the stone in shady areas feels cold and damp, then there is no point in continuing to climb with misplaced ambition; it is better to let the season fade away and to be content with a few leisurely outings on the remaining sunny days.

A possible structure for a season's training for freeclimbing is given in the table below (each training session has ten points, representing the full work load; thus one point represents one tenth of the time spent in training).

| | Components of workload | | | | | |
	Basic endurance	Maximum strength	Power	Strength-endurance	Technique	Flexibility
January		●●●	●●	●●	●	●●
February		●●	●●●	●●	●	●●
March		●	●●●	●●●	●	●●
April			●●	●●●●	●●	●●
May			●	●●●●●	●●●	●
June				●●●●●	●●●●	●
July	●			●●●●●	●●●	●
August	●●			●●●●	●●●	●
September	●●●	●		●●●	●●	●
October	●●●	●●		●●●	●	●
November	●●	●●●		●●	●	●●
December	●	●●●	●	●●	●	●●

Notes on table: Basic fitness is acquired through endurance runs, strength and flexibility exercises and work on the training equipment. This phase represents the transition from rock climbing to training in the gym. Dividing the annual schedule into shorter training cycles means that deadlines for achieving improvements in performance can be set, with individually selected performance peaks. The annual schedule can be further broken down into macro-cycles (4 to 6 weeks), micro-cycles (generally the same as the weekly training schedule) and the training session (the smallest planning unit). Thus the weekly training schedule of an ambitious amateur climber might contain the following elements:

Saturday and Sunday: intensive climbing with stretching exercises to conclude with on both days. Monday: rest day. Tuesday: intensive complementary training with or without climbing. Wednesday: rest day. Thursday: complementary training and climbing. Friday: rest day, possibly mental training.

This kind of training schedule is based on the extremely important principle of alternation between exertion and relaxation; regular participation in and a high level of commitment to a carefully planned programme will ensure great advances in performance levels.

Nutrition

If relative strength is crucially important in any particular sport, which is certainly the case with freeclimbing, then nutrition is also a factor in determining performance. A suitable diet will provide the energy required – particularly by supplying carbohydrates and considerably smaller quantities of fats and proteins – without excessive weight gain.

A so-called normal diet consists on average of 40 per cent carbohydrate, 40 per cent fat and 20 per cent protein. In other words, the average person consumes too much fat, too much protein, too much alcohol and too little carbohydrate. The diet of a well-nourished freeclimber, on the other hand, would consist of about 60 per cent carbohydrate, 25 per cent fat and 15 per cent protein. Moreover, he would make sure that his diet is rich in vitamins and minerals by eating wholefood products and fresh foods and drinking a suitable mineral water. His carbohydrate requirements can be supplied by the following foodstuffs: (wholemeal) bread and rolls, muesli, cereals, brown rice, wholemeal pasta, cakes and pastries, potatoes, vegetables, fruit, dried fruit and fruit juices.

This list makes it clear why most climbers seeking to improve their performance have now become vegetarians.

Success in freeclimbing does depend on a number of factors, not least on the planning of the advance up the rock face. Just starting to climb without any planning is usually unsuccessful, unless the climber is very lucky or is climbing a route that does not stretch her abilities. Thus thinking and acting strategically in the preparation phase and during the actual climb is important, particularly on routes that will push a climber to the limits of her abilities.

Getting ready

Apart from the long-term preparation that is the objective of the climber's training programme, specific preparation for a particular project becomes more important the closer the time comes. The first thing is to be clear what the aim of the project is. Are you intending to climb the route "on sight", to inspect it first, to rehearse the necessary moves or simply familiarize yourself with new sequences of moves? You should then try, by talking to people and reading climbing guides, to gather as much information about the route as possible. Before you start an ascent, you must be clear about the following things:

The path taken by the route, the degree of difficulty, the nature of the climb (whether it is biased towards power-endurance, maximum strength, etc.), the location of cruxes (i.e. the hard bits), the protection already in place and the protection that will have to be placed, the protection equipment required and the descent. The more detailed information you have, the more precisely you can plan the climb. Detailed descriptions of cruxes, resting spots, the sizes of nut required – to list just the most important aspects – are very useful.

Clipping in a ready-prepared quickdraw

The timing of the actual climb should be made dependent on external factors such as the weather, the position of the sun, mood, etc. The motivation of those involved plays an important role, since this is what releases reserves of ability. If you feel unwell or unmotivated for one reason or another, you will hardly be able to perform at your best.

The information you acquire should be turned over in your mind. You can prepare yourself mentally for the climb by carefully considering the sequences of moves involved and performing them in your head. If you have already inspected and tried out the route, mentally rehearsing each move over and over again can have a very beneficial effect.

If rough or sharp finger or hand cracks are expected, you can protect your hands from painful scrapes by taping them. You should make sure that the tape does not impair the circulation of blood through the hands and fingers or reduce their flexibility and strength. Tape can also be used to support the finger tendons in order to prevent injury.

Protection equipment should be sorted out and attached to the gear loops on your harness. Sorting and arranging the equipment carefully may well save you wasting a great deal of effort and energy, for example if the right nut for a particular placement is immediately to hand. Even clipping quickdraws on to the rope or your T-shirt will save valuable time when attaching the intermediate protection. However, the drag on the rope as it runs through a karabiner is greater than with a standard runner, so it is usually a good idea to confine this technique to the beginning of a pitch.

Before you begin to climb, warm up with a few exercises and a little light climbing. A good warm-up will help to prevent injury and also prepare the cardiovascular system and muscles for action.

Shortly before you begin the climb, tell your partner in as much detail as possible about your plans, so that protection errors can be eliminated. Then check your tie-in knot and protection equipment once again, rub your hands with chalk if necessary, clean the soles of your climbing shoes and start climbing.

The ascent

Now you have to put your plan into practice. However, it is not unknown for problems to crop up. They can usually be attributed to a lack of strength or technique or to inner tensions (fear). However, if you think and act tactically many of these situations can be overcome.

Switching techniques
Excessive use of a particular sequence of moves will make the muscle groups involved tire more quickly. If possible, you should use different types of grips, body positions, techniques, etc. If you cannot advance from a particular point, do not fall back on the same old techniques but try to work out some imaginative ideas for making further progress. Sometimes a solution can be found in this way, even if the same section of the route has been climbed by other freeclimbers in a different way.

Resting spots
Resting spots are climbing positions that a climber can use for recovery purposes. Fatigued muscles recover only if they are not working, or at least not working at more than 20 per cent of maximum strength. Since it is the arms that usually tire quickest, you should try to find positions in which they can be rested completely. Ideally, this should be a "no hand rest", a position in which the hands are not required at all. Such spots can typically be

Resting position

found in corner cracks (dihedrals) and cracks (in which the legs or body can be wedged). In other cases, imaginative use of foot hooks or knee jams is called for. If even these options are not available, at least try to take the strain off one arm. With the fingers pointing downwards in order to improve the circulation, shake the free hand vigorously; then change your handhold and do the same with the other arm. However, since many rest posi-tions still require the expenditure of some energy, the planned recovery period often turns out to be no such thing; instead, the climber simply wastes more energy and feels drained as a result. Less energy is generally expended in rest positions if the joints are moved to the maximum extension position. Consequently you must stretch your legs and the arm from which you are hanging as much as you possibly can.

Dipping into the chalkbag at a resting spot

Using chalk

The same thing can happen with chalk as with planned recovery periods. Whether from sheer force of habit or nervousness, climbers often make excessive use of chalk; as a result, the disadvantage of a loss of strength often outweighs the advantage to be gained from dry hands.

Dogging a route

Dogging a route is a frequently used tactic. It involves examining certain sections of the route with a top-rope belay before the actual ascent begins. The route is broken down into separate sequences of moves, none of which should be too long. Moves requiring the use maximum strength are avoided. Once a muscle has become overtired, a climber does not usually have sufficient strength left for a red-point ascent.

Speed of ascent

The speed of ascent should be steady and regular, each move following fluently from the last; a hectic pace is not called for. You should also be constantly on the lookout for resting spots from which you can inspect the next section of the route. Look for the next resting spot and then climb up to it, if possible without stopping. If difficulties occur when you are at the limits of your abilities, try to overcome them quickly. If you do not succeed, it is usually sensible to climb back to the last resting spot. After a short recovery period, try again and repeat the process until you succeed or give up.

Fear

Fear arises out of uncertainty. Uncertainty can be triggered by a feeling of exposure, failing strength, bad protection, loss of confidence in the safety chain or climbing difficulties at too high a location. The consequence is usually a vicious circle of inhibition, obstruction of the flow of movement and excessive energy expenditure.

If there is no rational reason to be afraid – if the anchors are "bombproof" and there is therefore no risk of injury in the event of a fall – a test jump often helps. In the best of cases, a deliberate jump reveals the fear of falling to be groundless. Once in a while, even the subconscious can be convinced. However, such tactics should be used only in very safe conditions.

Fear is nature's warning signal. Learning to cope with fear is essential for any climber, because in the long term climbing cannot be enjoyable unless you have confidence in your ability to deal with any situation that might arise. The best way of acquiring that confidence is to build it up during training and to select the routes you attempt judiciously.

Learning to cope with fear

Risks

There is a preconceived idea that freeclimbing is a dangerous sport. A common image is of prospective suicides, undaunted by death, working their way up a rock face, reaching dizzying heights and occasionally crashing to their death. However, such notions have nothing to do with modern freeclimbing. While climbers certainly used to suffer serious injuries as a result of falls, the injuries they sustain today are much more likely to be caused by excessive strain on fingers and arms as training programmes become ever more rigorous and routes ever more extreme. Nevertheless, the risk of a serious fall cannot be totally ruled out, although most freeclimbing routes on practice crags are very well protected. Thus accidents and stress injuries are the two negative aspects of freeclimbing.

Accidents

Falls are always a possibility in freeclimbing, but are not normally hazardous if the correct precautions are taken. However, if errors are made in placing protection, then the consequences may be tragic.

The failure of a piece of intermediate protection can dangerously extend the fall distance. Badly placed nuts and Friends or over-optimistic assessment of the reliability of a piton are the usual reasons for this. The length of a fall is often too long because too little intermediate protection, or even none at all, has been placed. This can be the cause of serious injury, particularly on alpine routes.

Other common mistakes include the incorrect use of waist belaying without protection for the belayer (too great a weight difference between the partners, belayer positioned too far away from the rock), belaying with a figure-of-eight descender without a glove on the brake hand, inadequate tie-in knots and running the rope directly through the sling in a top-rope set-up.

Injuries can occur if a climber has to jump off the rocks when bouldering without protection, particularly if he has climbed too high, does not prepare the jump properly or the terrain is unsuitable (boulders on the ground). The injuries most commonly sustained nowadays as a result of a fall involve the tendons and articular capsules of the fingers. If his feet give way unexpectedly beneath him, a climber's whole body weight can be left suspended from a few fingers before he eventually falls off the rock. The strain is usually taken by the ring or middle finger. Such injuries can be avoided not by gripping the rock tighter in a vain attempt to prevent the fall but by deliberately jumping off the rock at the right moment. The risk of injury is particularly high with dynamic moves and small finger-holes.

Other accidents, often serious ones, can also happen while abseiling. The failure of an anchor or errors in rope technique, due mainly to a lack of concentration after the exertions of climbing, are the usual causes. Most accidents that occur during the descent can also be attributed to fatigue and lack of concentration. Rock falls and sudden changes in the weather are hazards usually confined to alpine regions, although the risk of a rock fall cannot be ruled out on lower hills. Additional hazards on alpine climbs include lengthy approach and descent routes, often over difficult, unprotected terrain, and the total duration of any expedition, which can lead to dangerous situations if those involved lack adequate experience, stamina and equipment.

Stress injuries

The second group of injuries commonly sustained by freeclimbers are long-term injuries not caused by any one event. Since modern freeclimbing routes are particularly demanding on the arm muscles, stress injuries to tendon sheaths, tendon attachment points, articular capsules and nerves in the fingers, elbows and shoulders are fairly common occurrences. Most of these stress injuries are caused by climbing with the fingers tightly contracted. The consequent strain on the articular capsules can lead to chronic swelling. Painfully swollen finger joints, which in extreme cases can hardly be bent at all, are a typical symptom. If such symptoms are ignored, flail joints (joints with grossly excessive mobility) and arthrosis (disease of the joints) may set in. Climbing with the fingers tightly curled also places excessive strain on the tendon sheaths. The deflective and frictional forces on the flexing points of the tendon sheaths are so great that they can become inflamed if the technique is used frequently. Thorough warm-ups, stretching exercises for the finger muscles and using the extended grip position as much as possible will help to prevent injury.

The tendon sheaths in the forearm, and in particular the tendon attachment points at the elbows, are also exposed to frequent stress. Even the synovial bursae and tendon sheaths in the shoulders can be affected. In any event, you should take pain in any of these parts of the body seriously and respond by reducing the intensity of your training and climbing schedules. If you

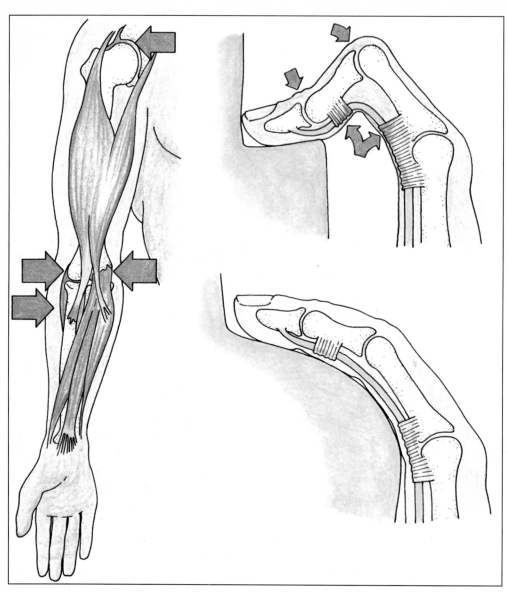

The arrows indicate neuralgic points on the arms and fingers that are exposed to the risk of injuries through overuse during climbing. Climbing with the fingers in the extended position (below right) helps to prevent such injuries to the hand

ignore pain, long-term, chronic damage may occur. Curiously, the antagonists of the overloaded parts – for example the finger tensor muscles or the pronators – are often affected as well. Obviously climbing also places strain on antagonists. However, they are not usually subject to special training and can be easily strained.

Types of Freedimbing

The individual inclinations of freeclimbers, the absence of strict regulations and the universal applicability of the basic climbing moves have led to the emergence of several different types of freeclimbing.

Bouldering

Bouldering involves climbing, usually without protection, on boulders or at the foot of climbs to a height where it is still safe to jump off. It is an excellent way of working out how to solve the most difficult climbing problems, which often consist of only two or three moves. The most imaginative sequences can emerge from such experimentation, which often lasts for weeks at a time. The American John Gill, who is said to be the founder of the bouldering movement, has even devised a separate rating system for bouldering, with grades from B1 to B3. B3 means that only one person to date has been able to climb a boulder with that grading.

Buildering

Buildering is, as the term suggests, climbing on buildings, walls, towers, monuments, etc. Apart from truly photogenic structures, the climbing of which usually attracts the wrath of the authorities or the owners, the piers of bridges or the walls of abandoned buildings are frequently used as a piece of sporting apparatus.

Bouldering

Buildering

Sport climbing

Sport climbing

This is defined as safe, gymnastic climbing with permanent protection for ultimate safety. All climbing is done without any artificial help, and the sole aim is to climb a single pitch without resting or falling. The climbing ethic is the same as freeclimbing, except that no anchors are placed or carried while climbing.

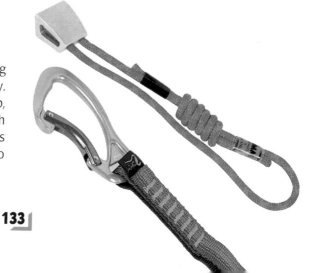

133

Alpine freeclimbing

Alpine freeclimbing

This is a sport of alpine regions (and not just of the Alps). It is a very taxing form of climbing because of the extra demands it makes of climbers.

Higher fitness levels

The access and descent routes and the length of climbs place additional demands on a climber's cardiovascular system and power-endurance.

Alpine experience

Additional risks (rock falls, holds that fail because of brittle rock, rapidly changing weather conditions), greater demands on protection technique (assessment of pitons, placement of a large number of anchors), complicated routes up long walls and climbing on relatively easy but rough and unprotected climbing terrain require a great deal of experience. In addition, skill in retreating techniques is also required.

Pressure of time

Alpine routes often take a whole day to climb, and climbers are constantly under pressure to complete a route before the light goes. There is certainly no time on alpine routes for spending hours dogging difficult moves at the limit of a climber's ability.

Additional equipment

Suitable equipment is required to deal with the more rigorous conditions. A pair of boots for the access and descent routes, rain gear, food and a first-aid kit, a chest harness and a helmet and adequate protection gear are just some of the items that will be needed. The additional equipment makes a rucksack necessary, which in turn make climbing all the more difficult.

Psychological factors

The constant exertion over long periods of time, the often overwhelming sense of exposure, the permanent pressure of time and the greater distances between pieces of protection place increased demands on climbers' morale. For all these reasons, climbers need to feel their way cautiously on demanding alpine routes.

Indoor climbing

A competitive sport, which is what freeclimbing has now become, needs all-weather training facilities. Environmental problems and the length of journeys to suitable climbing areas were also factors in the

Indoor climbing

development of artificial training walls, and a very wide variety of artificial holds and wall components is now commercially available. Multi-purpose "leisure and training walls" are springing up everywhere, in the stairwells of sports shops, in gyms and fitness centres and even in the cellars and basements of inveterate freeclimbers.

Competition climbing

A competitive sport needs some way of comparing performances. International competitions and rankings have now developed and events designed for media coverage held on artificial walls in sports halls have helped both to awaken public interest and to make possible objective comparisons of performance. Competition rules are constantly being altered and improved. The basic elements of competitive climbing are as follows. Qualifying rounds are held to select the best climbers for the final round. Climbing is on sight, so none of the participants is allowed to watch her fellow competitors climb the route. For this reason, competitors are often kept under lock and key in a warm-up room for hours on end to await their turn to climb. A precise route is defined, from which climbers may not deviate; the intermediate protection is usually already in place. The route has to be climbed in a given time without falls or artificial aids. If the climber falls, exceeds the time limit, uses an artificial aid or infringes the rules in any other way, then her performance is assessed on the basis of the highest point reached without breaking the rules. If several competitors complete the route, the victor is either the one with the fastest time or the winner of a play-off round held on a new route. There are now various international rankings, compiled like the international tennis rankings from the results of several competitions, which show how the best competition climbers compare with each other. Sponsorship, media hype and the requisite star personalities are all part of this new professional circus. A new and different dimension of the climbing ethic is being opened up.

Competition climbing

Artificial Climbing Walls

The different aims of rock climbing and indoor climbing make it clear that climbing on artificial walls is a new discipline with its own rules; this was further reinforced by the introduction of sport climbing as a demonstration event at the 1992 Olympic Games.

Comparison of these different aims is revealing. In rock climbing, the climber attempts to reach a particular goal (e.g. the top of a crag) along the route of least resistance. That route is defined by the first person to climb it; he takes account of natural features while at the same time choosing the shortest path offering the fewest difficulties for the climber. For climbers tackling the route subsequently, the choice of technique is irrelevant; even for the crux, or most difficult section of the route, they may adopt a completely different technique from that used by the first person to climb it.

The aim of indoor climbing is also to reach a defined goal, but the technique to be adopted is defined by the person constructing the route.

The designer of a route on an artificial wall will seldom choose the shortest path; his aim is rather to make the route as long and as interesting as possible. Through careful placement of foot and handholds, he will try to make the route as difficult as possible. So clearly, the aims of rock and indoor climbing can even be said to contradict each other.

Foot jamming on a roof

The various forms of indoor climbing are: technical climbing, bouldering, climbing against the clock, speed climbing and a competitive discipline that is a hybrid form of route climbing and climbing against the clock. The aim of technical climbing is to climb a defined route of variable difficulty using the same sequence of moves. The level of difficulty is increased either by making the holds smaller or by gradually increasing the extent to which the wall overhangs while leaving the holds unchanged.

The aim of climbing against the clock is to climb as far as possible within a given time.

Speed climbing is a discipline in which the time taken to reach a goal is recorded on a stopwatch. In competition climbing, the criterion is the highest point reached without falling. If two or more climbers reach the same point or complete the route successfully, then the time taken is used to decide the winner.

However, clearly defined rules and prescribed sequences of moves are not the only differences between indoor climbing and traditional sport climbing; there are also considerable differences in technique. The main difficulty on a vertical rock face is usually the

from their own training sessions. A comparable hold on a natural rock face would be too risky for dynamic moves, since the climber is unaware either of its exact shape or of its surface texture, which changes constantly with the weather conditions.

One technique provides a particularly clear demonstration of the difference between indoor and rock climbing: foot jams on roofs. One of the characteristics of difficult roofs on artificial walls is the predominance of relatively large handholds spaced at relatively wide intervals. Since good handholds also make the best footholds, the number of holds is very low but they are of such good quality that they can be easily held with one foot on top of the hold and the other on the bottom jamming the top foot in place. In this way, the outstretched body can be held in a stable, two-point position, leaving one hand free to grip a handhold some distance away. Such situations are extremely rare on natural roofs.

small size of the available holds. However, this is not the case on artificial walls, because manufacturers are unable, for technical reasons, to produce holds below a certain size. The main difficulties on artificial walls are then, the extreme positions achieved and the length of individual moves.

Indoor climbing provides many good opportunities for practising dynamic moves. In order to minimize the risk of injury, artificial holds are ergonomically shaped, which makes the quality of any particular hold easier to judge. Indeed, climbers are often familiar with the holds

How to build a practice wall

The size and type of room

Do-it-yourself is not everybody's favourite activity, but very effective climbing walls can be built relatively simply, provided you plan carefully and work systematically. In order to avoid disappointment, you should begin by building up a precise picture of the premises and considering the possible locations for a climbing wall. It would be a big mistake to have too fixed an idea of the kind of wall you want to build and to try to fit into your home by any means possible. Of course a practice wall is a functional piece of equipment, but the nature of the available space must be taken into account in designing and constructing it. Three possible locations are described below, together with various suggestions for incorporating a climbing wall into them.

Living room or cellar

It is frequently said of climbers that "all the good ones have their own climbing wall in the cellar". The idea of building a climbing wall in the cellar seems to be linked to the fact that, at the beginning of the health and fitness craze, all sporting activities at home were shifted into the hobby-room, i.e. into the cellar. If the cellar is well heated, it makes a very suitable location for a climbing wall; under no circumstances, however, should you train in cold, unheated rooms.

A climbing wall could also be built in a living room, and could even be made into an attractive feature. However, you should bear in mind that the use of chalk will make the apartment dirty and impair air quality. The ideal locations for a practice wall in an apartment are the entrance hall or corridor. The basic requirement for building a wall is a simple rectangular space with an average height of between 2.4 and 3.2 metres.

Loft or attic apartment

Such apartments usually have sloping ceilings that can be incorporated into the design of a climbing wall. Uninsulated lofts are very problematic in winter and are only of limited value as training rooms. In order to avoid injury, the space underneath any permanently installed overhangs must be free of obstructions. There is no point, for example, in climbing up a sloping wall if there is a desk underneath, since premeditated jumps are as much a part of training as uncontrolled falls. A word of warning for beginners is appropriate at this point. If you are thinking of just screwing a few holds into the wall for occasional practice, in the belief that you cannot possibly fall off, think again. Many people have done the same thing and lived to regret it. You must plan for the possibility of controlled and uncontrolled jumps and make sure there is enough free space.

An outside wall of a building

The most important criterion for constructing a practice wall on the outside of your house is the weather conditions. It is best to choose a location on the most sheltered side, preferably with some sort of roof over it. If artificial holds are exposed continuously to rain, moss starts to grow on them, making them slippery and unusable. However, one of the big advantages of outside walls is that you can design very high routes that can stretch over several storeys. It is possible, though not always sensible, to attach hand and footholds to virtually any wall. For concrete walls, there are metal cavity plugs, while plastic plugs are available for solid brick and limestone walls. However, climbing walls on cavity walls will have to be glued or cemented in place. As this can be a very expensive business you should only undertake the work if you are totally sure that you will use the wall.

Some basic types of wall with examples

The first decision that has to be made is whether the hand and footholds should be attached directly to the supporting wall or to some sort of support panel. If the first option seems at first sight the simpler one, it may actually require far more time and energy than other, apparently more complicated approaches. It should be possible on a good practice wall to move holds around and, ideally, to tilt the wall as well. Both of these requirements can be fulfilled only by attaching the holds to a support panel. Even if you decide on a less sophisticated approach, you should still bear in mind that it is easier to screw holds into a wooden panel and then attach the whole panel to the supporting wall with a few bolts than to have to drill a separate hole for each hold.

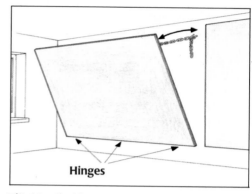

Tiltable climbing wall for living rooms

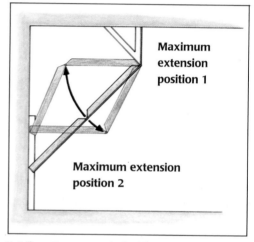

Folding, three-panel climbing wall

Living room or cellar

The best way of using a normal living room for this purpose is to install a tilting practice wall that takes up little space. In the closed position, the wall will only jut out about 8 cm into the room. When tilted, it is supported on chains. The minimum width for the support panel is 160 cm.

If there is more space available and the wall does not always have to be closed up after use, then three separate panels can be joined with hinges and pulled out separately for use. This is the simplest way of constructing an adjustable wall that can be used in many different positions to simulate sheer or inclined rock faces, and even roofs.

Loft or attic apartment

If the room already has a sloping ceiling, you should incorporate it into your design. Rigid walls can be as useful as tiltable ones. If you are installing a tiltable practice wall, it is best to mount the hinges along the top rather than the bottom edge, in contrast to the method adopted for a vertical wall.

An outside wall of a building

Height rather than variability is the watchword here. Carefully planned routes should make it possible to use extensive sequences of moves. In this case, it is quite appropriate to attach the hand and footholds directly to the brickwork. Careful placement and symmetrical sequences of holds will help to make individual sections of the wall more durable. From 3 metres upwards, protection points are essential!

Choosing the type best suited to your purposes

Which of these five types is most suitable depends not only on the location but also on the intended use. If all you want to do is climb up the side of your house occasionally in the evening sun, all you need to do is attach some holds to an outside wall. On the other hand, wooden panels with holes drilled to form a grid pattern and then fixed directly to the brickwork are much more suitable for systematic training. By spending a little more money on hinges and a wooden frame to strengthen the panels, you will be able to install a tiltable wall that will be even more versatile.

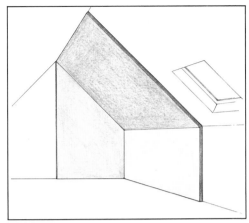

Rigid wall in an attic apartment

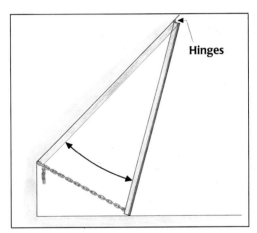

Hinges

Tiltable wall in a loft

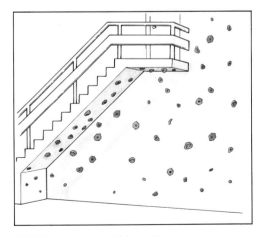

Climbing on an outside wall

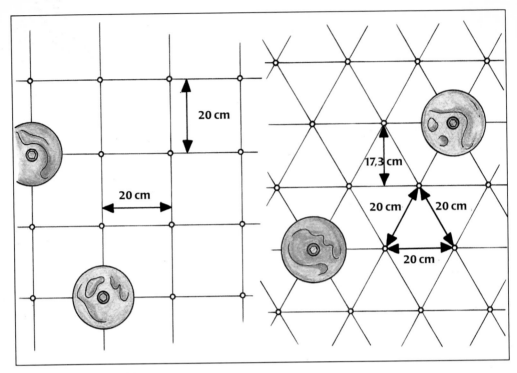

90° grid (l.), 60° grid (r.)

Deciding on the design with some examples

Panels with grid patterns

The recommended material for the support panels is multi-ply at least 15 mm thick. Beech ply is particularly strong and you can get away with a minimum thickness of 12 mm, but it has the disadvantage of being heavy and is also very expensive. For safety reasons, no other kind of board should be used; chipboard is particularly to be avoided, since the weakness of its structure makes it unreliable, and it has already been the cause of several serious accidents.

There are two kinds of grid pattern that can be used: a 90° grid or a 60° grid. You should also establish the maximum possible number of drill holes per square metre. If you choose a square grid pattern with the holes 20 cm apart, you will have 16 attachment points per square metre, which is perfectly adequate. The 60° grid pattern with the holes 20 cm apart will give you 23 attachment points per square metre.

Tiltable wall made of panels strengthened with wooden frames

With a tiltable wall, the pulling forces on the wooden panels would cause them to twist if they were not strengthened. The panel should be made of multi-ply as described above, while the best material for the frame is softwood. The frame should be not only screwed to the panel but also glued in place. Otherwise, enjoyment of your new practice wall may well be short-lived.

Each panel should be fully enclosed within a frame. If the surface area is greater than 1 m²,

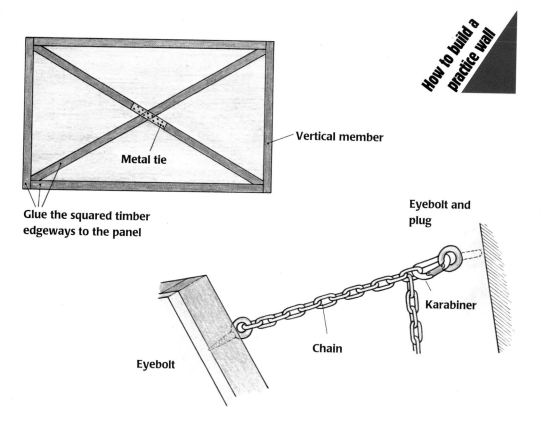

Vertical member

Metal tie

Glue the squared timber edgeways to the panel

Eyebolt and plug

Karabiner

Chain

Eyebolt

a diagonal brace will be needed to prevent the board from bulging under load when tilted outwards. With panels up to 2 m² in area, the braces should be at least 40 mm deep and attached edgeways to the panel. With panels more than 2 m² in area, the use of squared timber is recommended (60 x 80 mm or 80 x 80 mm).

Individual panels more than 3 m wide and 2 m high have proved to be impractical. Large areas should, therefore, be subdivided into smaller segments. Ideally, these tiltable segments should be attached to the wall with hinges about 30 to 40 cm above the floor. Use heavy-duty hinges screwed to the side of the frame and at intervals of no more than a metre along its lower edge. In living rooms of normal height, the wall may extend right up to ceiling height. Attach the anchor chain with

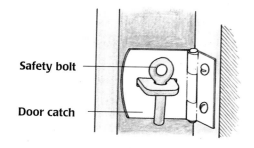

Safety bolt

Door catch

Diagonal braces (top left)
Detail of the tiltable wall: The wall supported by a chain in the tilted position (middle)
Secured to the wall (bottom)

an eyebolt as high up as possible on the side member of the frame. The chain should also be attached to the wall as high up as possible, though still within reach. In order to keep the climbing wall flush with the wall when stowed away, several door catches can be screwed to the side of the frame.

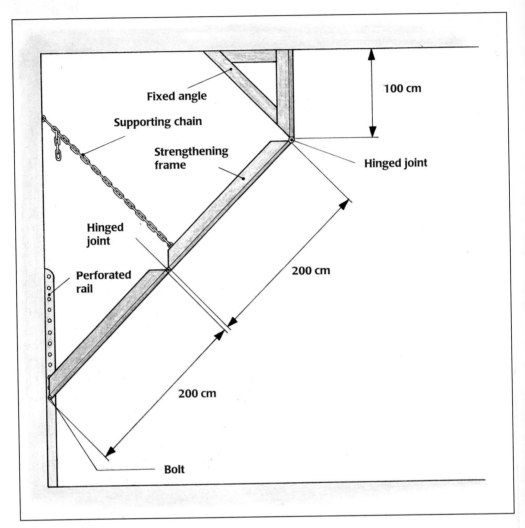

Details of a folding climbing wall

Fully adjustable wall with overhang

Three panels of equal width are hinged together; the top one is fixed to the ceiling at right angles, while the bottom one can be moved along a rail fixed to the side wall. Once set up in this way, the wall can be pivoted around the two joints and fixed in a variety of different positions. The middle panel can be attached to the wall with two chains, while the bottom one is held in place with a bolt pushed through one of the holes in the rail. The size of the individual panels is a matter of personal taste, but experience shows that the most useful width is about 200 cm. The length of the individual panels should be calculated in such a way as to allow for a range of different maximum extension positions. A ratio of 2 : 2 : 1 (lower : middle : top board) has proved to be optimal. Multi-ply with a minimum thickness of 17 mm can be used for all three panels; plywood less than 17 mm thick will have to be strengthened with a wooden frame.

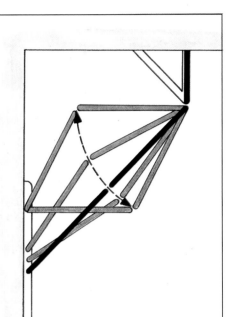

Possible positions

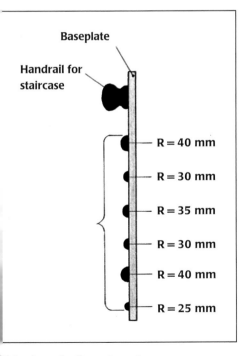

Baseplate

Handrail for staircase

R = 40 mm

R = 30 mm

R = 35 mm

R = 30 mm

R = 40 mm

R = 25 mm

Side view of a finger board

Hang boards

Hang boards are not actually climbing walls, but should be mentioned at this point for the sake of completeness. They consist of a base-board about 100 x 140 cm in size on which rounded knobs of wood of various sizes (20 to 60 mm in depth) are mounted. Circular pieces of timber, ranging in thickness from broom handle to fencing post and split in half lengthways, are particularly suitable for this purpose. Because of the risk of injury from wood splinters, it is advisable to ask a joiner to prepare the timber. These rounded pieces of wood are particularly good for training on because you will not have to contract your fingers too much, thereby minimising the risk of stress injuries. The hang board should be mounted some distance from the wall so that you can hang freely from it.

General advice on installation

When fixing the mountings to the brickwork, particular attention should be paid to the solidity of the plugs and screws. Metal cavity plugs are suitable for concrete walls, while for lighter materials plastic plugs in metric thread sizes are available. The screws should have a metric thread and a strength rating of at least 8.8. Wood screws purchased in DIY stores are just not strong enough! Most of the accidents on home-made climbing walls are caused by inadequate fixings.

Preparing the surfaces and attaching the holds

The panels should be prepared for use by roughening the surfaces. Special plastic panels coated with corundum are manufactured industrially for use in competition climbing. Unfortunately, it is impossible to produce such coatings at home, but it is now possible to buy competition climbing panels by the metre. However, those wishing to save money can use acrylic paint (emulsion), which is best applied with a large lambswool roller. With a little skill and generous application of the paint, you should succeed in creating a rough and durable surface. Left in its original state, plywood is a totally unsuitable surface for climbing practice, since the special rubber soles of climbing shoes would not adhere to it. If you are prepared to put yourself to the trouble of making a practice wall, there is no point in spoiling the job by saving money on the most important part, i.e. the surface.

In order to attach the holds, threaded sleeves are pushed from the back of the panel through the drill holes. They can also be hammered through, but they usually bend out of line slightly in the process. To make the job easier, you can make yourself a handy tool by screwing several nuts on to a bolt and attaching as big a washer as possible. Use your improvised device to pull the sleeves carefully through the drill holes from the front. The use of threaded inserts, which are sometimes recommended, has proved particularly hazardous, since they can all too easily be pulled out of the panel.

The placement of foot and handholds should be planned carefully and allow a climber to take several different routes up the wall.

If the routes are to be organized in a way that will make a real contribution to training, they should be clearly divided into handholds and footholds. So the lower part of the wall should have only footholds, while the upper part should have only handholds. The difference is that footholds are considerably smaller, while handholds should not have any sharp edges.

Organizing a training programme

Climbing on artificial climbing walls can be a lot of fun. However, sheer amusement should not be allowed to get in the way of purposeful training. You should not forget to warm up properly, for example, nor should you start off immediately with difficult sequences of moves. Climbing predetermined routes will take up most of your time, but there are many ways of making training more interesting. In order to define a route, you can either paint handholds in different colours or give each handhold a number and then climb using a particular sequence of numbers or colours.

If your training sessions become a little boring, try livening them up by introducing some new exercises. You could practise twisting your body on its own axis as a means of improving coordination and balance. Or you could set an upper limit on handholds in order to practise lowering your centre of gravity quickly. And finally, you could climb certain sections against the clock, in order to improve dexterity and nimbleness.

To finish with, here are two climbing games:

First climb a predefined route with the wall in its vertical position. After each climb, increase the angle of tilt somewhat to form an overhang. Anyone who falls off is out of the game. The winner is the last one remaining player who successfully climbs the route with the wall at its steepest angle of incline.

In the second game, each hold on a sharply overhanging wall can be used only once. After a maximum pause of ten seconds, the

Climbing on a home-made practice wall

climber has to move on, using the left and right hands alternately. The person who finds the most suitable route with the best resting points usually records the longest time and thus wins the game. Depending on performance levels, both the angle of tilt and the permitted resting time can be altered. Have fun!

Index

A WARD LOCK BOOK

First published in the UK 1997
by Ward Lock
Wellington House
125 Strand
London
WC2R 0BB

A Cassell Imprint

Distributed in the United States
by Sterling Publishing Co., Inc.
387 Park Avenue South, New York, NY 10016-8810
A British Library Cataloguing in Publication Data block for this book may be obtained from the British Library

ISBN 0 7063 7498 3
Photos: Bernhard Thum, Nuremberg, except:
Archiv Dieter Hasse, Großhelfendorf/Hörig: p. 9
Franz Hefner, Nuremberg: p. 11
Gerd Heidorn, Munich: p. 18, p. 56
Matthias Pausch, Munich: p. 64, p. 108
Archiv Schlager & Strobl, Eurasburg: p. 22 (middle), p. 22 (bottom), p. 24/Alex Haigh: p. 134
Thomas Strobl, Münsing: p. 27, p. 61 (right), p. 77 (top left)
Detlef Schumacher, Cologne: p. 132 (bottom)
Uli Wiesmeier, Großweil: p. 10, p. 39, p. 40, p. 42, p. 45, p. 53 (top left), p. 58, p. 62, p. 102, p. 119, p. 126 (top)
Martin Zeller, Munich: p. 132 (top), p. 135
Illustrations: Georg Sojer, Ruhpolding

Translation: Andrew Wilson for First Edition Translations Ltd, Great Britain

Typesetting: Squires Graphics for First Edition Translations Ltd, Great Britain

Printed and bound by Pozzo Gros Monti S.p.A. - Turin - Italy